GROW-BED GARDENING

GROW-BED GARDENING
T.M.

By
Jacob R. Mittleider, Ph.D.
Originator of "Grow-Box" Gardening
T.M.
Author of
More Food From Your Garden
Food for Everyone

Published by
Woodbridge Press / *Santa Barbara, California*
®

1992

Published and distributed by

Woodbridge Press Publishing Company
Post Office Box 6189
Santa Barbara, California 93160

Copyright © 1986 by Jacob R. Mittleider

Library of Congress Cataloging in Publication Data

Mittleider, Jacob R.
   Grow-bed gardening.

   Includes index.
   1. Vegetable gardening. 2. Raised bed gardening.
I. Title.
SB321.M645 1968   635   85-31475
ISBN 0-88007-144-3

Contents

Dedication

In preparing the manuscript for this book my thoughts often went back several years to the publication of an earlier book, *Food for Everyone.*

Dr. Andrew Nelson was an author and editor. And even though he had plans and a schedule to publish nearly a score of books of his own he revised that schedule and devoted his skill and energy to the laborious task of editing and organizing the materials for *Food for Everyone.*

The work required many months and there were serious obstacles. But, after Dr. Nelson had decided the book was needed and it was up to him to make it available, he never wavered or faltered.

Little did I realize then the foresight Dr. Nelson possessed and the extent of the influence the book would have around the world and on myself.

Dr. Nelson's dedication and expertise is seen throughout *Food for Everyone,* which is still as popular today as when the first edition was printed. His dedication has been a continuing inspiration to me and, to a large degree, I owe to him the progress achieved in my work to the present time.

Therefore, I am pleased to dedicate this book to Dr. Andrew Nelson—a man of sterling character whose influence lives on.

The Author

Testimonials

Testimonials to the striking effectiveness of the Mittleider Method in both home and commercial gardens pour in from all over the world. Some, from the more than 30 countries in which the Method has been demonstrated, have appeared in earlier books. Here are some additional ones from recent demonstration areas.

C. D. Promnitz
Provincial Agricultural Officer
Matabeleland, South, Zimbabwe, Africa
From a Commencement Address to graduates of the Mittleider Training
  Course:

To the trainees who have had a unique opportunity to study at first hand a programme of food production which really works. . . . This system is a combination of hard work, common sense, and "loving care" all put together by one man, Dr. Mittleider. . . . [I have been] completely converted by the simplicity and soundness of the system and above all the results. . . .

Dr. Mittleider, no matter how short or how long your stay in this country you have lit a torch which will burn for a long time.

Sandy, Utah, Central Stake
President Charles A. Jones
In Behalf Of The Church of Jesus Christ of Latter-Day Saints.

Dear Mitt:

I am pleased to write this letter concerning our experience using the Mittleider Method of growing a large variety of fresh vegetables for the L.D.S. Welfare System. . . .

My personal feelings and those shared by my associates are, that the Mittleider Method is a most enjoyable means of growing food. . . . The results are fantastically more rewarding than I have ever had in my 30 years of growing vegetables by conventional means. The production is heavier, quality higher, and the results more dramatic in every way.

I am pleased to recommend the Mittleider Method to everyone for pleasure or profit.

National Courier Correspondent
Dr. William Willoughby

WASHINGTON:—Dr. Mittleider knows one thing that can change the face of the earth, and he's trying to get someone to listen. No matter how poor man, or man's soil is, if there's a way to get water to it, with only a plot of ground 20' × 100', a man can feed his family better than it has ever been fed before. . . .

He has proven his claims in just about every type of adverse situation in the world. . . .

The Idaho baker-turned-agricultural wizard, specializes in turning what is known as "devil-land" into unbelievably productive land. The beauty of the program is that the transformation can take place anywhere from three to six months, with food to spare and to share for the effort. . . .

"There's no reason why there is a single person in the world who has to go to bed hungry."

Utah Navajo-Baa Hane

Dr. Mittleider has shown in his demonstration garden project at Halchita that it is possible to grow a successful garden despite poor soil conditions. . . .

The . . . garden was started in June. In four weeks, the barren, rocky plot was transformed into a lush garden that has produced a variety of crops. . . .

The garden stirred considerable interest throughout the area.

Those visiting the project who are familiar with the landscape around Halchita stare in disbelief at the seeming oasis that has materialized. . . . Neat rows of green vegetables are separated by walkways that allow easy access to the plants. A variety of harvested vegetables are being sold. . . .

At Halchita, Mittleider used existing soil to prove that even poor soil, strong winds, and high temperatures are not obstacles to limit production of successful crops if the right techniques are used.

Plans are being laid to expand the project into a full-scale training program . . . to bring improved gardening projects to Navajos throughout the Utah strip.

San Juan Record
By Marsha Keele

In the middle of Monument Valley's desert area, . . . lush vegetation is flourishing as part of a scientific garden demonstration sponsored by Utah Navajo Development Council (UNDC).

Dr. Jacob Mittleider . . . has shown that food can be produced "in the world's worst soil."

The goal of UNDC is to involve local residents in continuing the garden and implementing the method in their own home plots.

The Chronicle
Bulawayo, Zimbabwe, Africa

Dr. Mittleider is performing what many people would have thought to be humanly impossible—developing a vegetable garden on the infertile sandy soil around Solusi . . . College.

[The] "miracle" demonstration plot was begun . . . to train people from various parts of Zimbabwe to grow their own food without relying on foreign, expensive imports.

W. W. Glover
Utah Navajo Development Council
Blanding, Utah
Associate Executive Director

Dear Dr. Mittleider:

Thank you for being willing to give of your time and energies this past summer in raising a successful demonstration garden at Halchita. After this experience, UNDC is committed more than ever to the goal of transferring your knowledge and expertise in gardening to the Navajo people. . . .

In evaluating the . . . project, I feel that it was very successful. Dr. Baha Billy, the Navajo agronomist and instructor for the Navajo Community College was also very favorable in his evaluation of the garden. . . . I feel that Dr. Billy's greatest compliment and endorsement of the project was his statement that he would like to participate in the training programs next year.

Kirtland, N.M.
Baha Billy, Ph.D., Soil Scientist
Halchita Garden Evaluation Report:

The garden shown to me . . . was very impressive. It is an excellent example of what can be done if the right combination of talent and agricultural resources are brought together for crop production.

Washington, D.C.,
Adventist Review

Elliott Dima, . . . a graduate of the 12-week course in scientific vegetable gardening at Solusi College, Bulawayo, returned to visit in August. . . .

Mr. Dima . . . is an instructor for the Zimbabwean Government Agency Agritex. He brought with him 78 farmers and gardeners from the Plumtree area. . . . Mr. Dima studied gardening under Jacob Mittleider and estimates that about 300 farmers in the Plumtree area have become familiar with the Mittleider Method and are using it quite successfully.

Utah Navajo Industries
Blanding, Utah
Dineh Staff

We would like to express our appreciation for sharing your knowledge of agriculture with us. . . . We watched you work and also watched your crops grow to maturity. It is amazing to know what a man's time can accomplish. . . . You have taught us a lot.

Mr. Curtis Jones
Bluff, Utah

It was a pleasure to work with Dr. Mittleider in raising a commercial crop of melons in Bluff, Utah.

I learned a lot from him and will be able to utilize it in future operations.

Dr. Mittleider is knowledgeable and interested in helping others to succeed in agriculture.

Amazing Food Yields From Mittleider Grow-Beds

Did you know a plot of ground only 50′ × 35′ planted in Mittleider Grow-Beds can yield any of these . . . ?

1. 1900 pounds potatoes

2. 700 pounds beans

3. 3,312 ears of corn

4. 936 heads of cabbage (3#)

5. 936 heads broccoli (1½#)

6. 936 heads cauliflower (2#)

7. 936 heads lettuce (1½#)

8. 700 pounds peas

9. 190 plants zucchini squash (6#)

10. 570 plants cantaloupe (6#)

11. 380 plants watermelon (18#)

12. 380 plants banana squash (20#)

13. 666 plants tomatoes (8#)

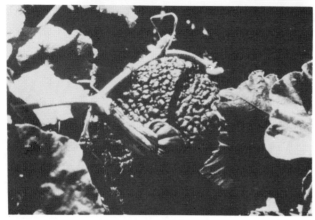

14. 380 plants acorn squash (10#)

A Typical Grow-Bed Garden

Divide the 50′ × 35′ area mentioned above into 10 plots (beds) 18″ wide × 30′ long, with 3½′ wide aisles between beds.

Each narrow *bed* should contain *two* rows of plants:

Potatoes . . .

. . . and corn are planted 8″ apart in the rows.

Beans . . .

. . . and peas are planted 1″ apart.

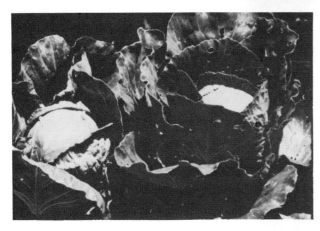

Cabbage, lettuce, broccoli, and cauliflower are planted 14″ apart.

Squashes and melons, 20″ apart.

Tomatoes are planted 8″ apart in the row.

To be able to harvest two crops with an assortment of the foods listed above in one season it is important to transplant well-grown potted plants in the Grow-Beds.

A Suggested Planting List for the First Planting and the estimated yield:

1	bed potatoes	(105#)	@21¢	=	$ 22.05
1	bed beans	(40#)	@79¢	=	31.60
1	bed peas	(39#)	@59¢	=	23.01
½	bed broccoli 26 plants	(1½#)	@59¢	=	23.01
½	bed lettuce 26 plants	(1½#)	@59¢	=	23.01
½	bed cauliflower 26 plants	(2#)	@39¢	=	20.28
½	bed cabbage 26 plants	(3#)	@29¢	=	22.62
1	bed sweetcorn 184 plants = 106 ears		@12¢	=	12.72
1	bed zucchini 20 plants	(6#)	@69¢	=	82.80
1	bed banana squash	(20#)	@12¢	=	96.00
1	bed canteloupes 60 plants	(3#)	@27¢	=	48.60
½	bed watermelons 40 plants	(16#)	@12¢	=	76.80
1	bed tomatoes 92 plants	(8#)	@69¢	=	507.84
10					$990.34

In addition, a Second Planting is made of the following:

1	bed potatoes	(105#)	@21¢	=	$ 22.05
1	bed beans	(39#)	@79¢	=	30.81
1	bed peas	(39#)	@59¢	=	23.01
½	bed broccoli 26 plants	(1½#)	@59¢	=	23.01
½	bed lettuce 26 plants	(1½#)	@59¢	=	23.01
½	bed cauliflower 26 plants	(2#)	@39¢	=	20.28
½	bed cabbage 26 plants	(3#)	@29¢	=	22.62
1	bed sweetcorn 184 plants @10¢ per ear			=	18.40
6					$183.19

ONE SEASON'S RETAIL $1,173.53

Total number beds for one season: 16

Fixed expenses to produce the two crops:

50	pounds gypsum (or other lime)	@22¢	= $	11.00
50	pounds fertilizer (preplant)	@42¢	=	21.00
150 pounds fertilizer (Weekly Feed)		@42¢	=	63.00
Seed, including potato and tomato (estimated)			=	35.00
Water (estimated)			=	50.00
		TOTAL FIXED EXPENSES		$180.00

Capital investment outlay:

1	shovel	$ 9.00
1	rake	9.00
1	hoe	9.00
1	75 feet of garden hose	32.00
1	30 gallon drum	9.00
1	3 gallon pail	4.35
1	watering wand	7.00
1	8′ × 14′ greenhouse with table	400.00
	500 2″ plastic square pots	15.00
	500 3″ plastic square pots	18.00
	100 6″ plastic square pots	20.00
2	bags 4 cu. ft., perlite	9.00
2	bags 4 cu. ft., forest mulch	8.00
		$549.35

Depreciation, one fifth per year:	109.87

Expenses for one season's crops, excluding labor:	$289.87
Cost per bed to produce the crops ($289.87 ÷ 16) =	18.12
Income per bed from crops ($1,173.53 ÷ 16) =	73.35

A list of potted vegetable plants needed to plant the crops listed above:

2 beds potatoes, 184	2 beds sweetcorn, 184
2 beds beans, 388	1 bed tomatoes, 92
2 beds peas, 388	¼ bed banana squash, 20
1 bed broccoli, 52	¼ bed acorn squash, 20
1 bed lettuce, 52	¼ bed zucchini squash, 20
1 bed cauliflower, 52	½ bed cantaloupes, 20
1 bed cabbage, 52	½ bed watermelons, 20

Note: The success of an adventure-packed gardening program depends on planting fresh seed of high-percent germination . . .

. . . and transplanting healthy seedlings into pots filled with clean soil materials . . .

. . . to produce strong plants with heavy roots 4 to 6 weeks before the weather permits transplanting into the Grow-Beds.

Buying potted plants from nurseries or other retail outlets is a good second choice, but there are two disadvantages: 1. The cash outlay to purchase the plants desired can be high; and, 2. frequently the plants are too small, too large, or of poor quality, or may not be available when needed.

Optional Planting from Seed:

If land is available and the growing season permits, crops such as beans, peas, and some others can be grown from seed planted right in the Grow-Beds or in the standard-size Grow-Boxes described in *More Food From Your Garden.*

Here's How!

A. *Standard-size 5' × 30' beds* (See *More Food From Your Garden*):

Mark off the plots. Clear the ground and till the soil.

Spread the lime and preplant fertilizers.

Prepare a good seedbed.

Mark the beds for proper row spacing and cut furrows across the beds.

Scatter the seed ½ to 1″ apart in the row.

Take a garden tool such as a "dutch hoe," and cover the seed.

After planting, water the beds to settle the loose soil.

B. *Grow-Beds 18″ wide × 30′ Long:*

Prepare the narrow beds for planting.

Cut furrows for two rows of seed in each bed.

Place the seed 1″ apart in the rows.   Cover the seed with coarse sand.

After the beds are planted, water adequately and keep moist while seeds are sprouting.

What Are Grow-Beds?

Grow-Beds are narrow strips of ground prepared for intensive food growing.

The plots are generally 18″ wide × 30′ long.

But the length can vary—it may be 15′ long, for example.

. . . or it may be 100′ long!

What is of real importance is that the Grow-Beds should be level.

Grow-Beds are successful: "None need stand in the field amidst the sad wreck of their hopes."

. . . "False witness is borne condemning land . . .

. . . which if properly worked would yield rich returns."

A real problem:

Around the world millions of people are underfed . . .

. . . and many are even starving.—

This is not because land is unavailable;

. . . there are millions of garden-size plots lying dormant nearly everywhere but they are not being used.

There is a solution:

"Agriculture should be advanced with scientific knowledge."

"Persons of proper ability should make a study of the soil; . . .

. . . learn how to plant, . . .

. . . how to cultivate, . . .

. . . how to fertilize, . . .

. . . how to water . . .

. . . and gather in the harvest, [then] more encouraging results would be seen."

After many years of research, growing crops under unusual conditions, a simple method of growing crops has been developed.

Now, with Grow-Beds you can harvest bigger yields with less hard work.

You can grow more food in less space, . . .

. . . more easily than you think. HOW? . . .

In Grow-Beds . . .

or, narrow framed Grow-Boxes (See *More Food from Your Garden*).

Again, What are Grow-Beds?

They are narrow, slightly raised, and leveled strips of land.

Usually 18″ wide × 30′ long, but not always. The length can vary—but not the width.

No compost, no manure, or other organic or synthetic soil ammendments are used. . . .

. . . just the raw, virgin soil.

(If wooden frames are used, as in the Grow-Box method, they are filled with a special soil medium such as 40% peat-moss, 40% sawdust, 20% sand.)

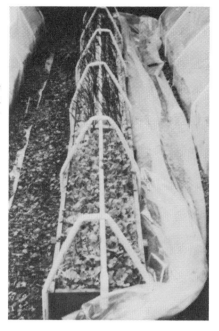

The balanced essential nutrients are spread evenly over the Grow-Bed area.

Grow-Beds can be made nearly anywhere.

They are not limited by poor soil, . . .

. . . saline (salty) soil, . . .

. . . hard or pulverized sandstone, . . .

. . . rocky soil, . . .

. . . or hilly terrain.

29

Plants thrive in almost any climate, . . .

. . . whether hot or dry, . . .

. . . moderate, . . .

. . . temperate, . . .

. . . or cold.

The Grow-Beds can be fitted with simple "A" frames made of plastic pipe.

When the "A" frames are covered with clear plastic the Grow-Bed is an inexpensive miniature greenhouse.

This is a welcome protection from wind and cold for early crops.

Nearly all vegetable crops can be grown in the Grow-Beds.

These potatoes grew in just 8 weeks. They were never cultivated or ridged—only fed and watered.

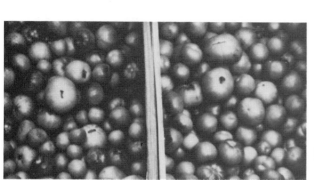

Delicious, ripe tomatoes.

Juicy, crisp red beets.

Sweet, well-shaped watermelons . . .

Ears of sweetcorn, filled out completely.

Tender stringless beans, . . .
. . . and the vines are loaded!

Sweet carrots.

Cabbage.

Long, straight seedless cucumbers.

The Grow-Beds provide the key . . .

. . . to make use of the poorest land, . . .

. . . to support close planting and heavy bearing.

That means maximum food in minimal space.

Grow-Beds can be used nearly anywhere—on a city lot, . . .

. . . a family garden, . . .

. . . a school farm, ... a resident home, . . .

. . . a community project, . . .

. . . or a commercial operation.

Really, any size project is possible.

Weeds, if they occur, are of little consequence.

Land barren and idle,
can be made to produce . . .

. . . crop after crop, year after year . . .

. . . and keep right on producing an abundance of food—

Success is assured because nothing is left to chance.

Why Grow-Bed Gardens?

The information in this book—on growing fresh vegetables to meet the needs of the family with a surplus to share or sell—is the outgrowth of many years of research and experimentation in more than two score countries around the world under most unusual and varied circumstances, most recently in Africa, Southern Utah, and Trinidad, Tobago, W.I..

Nearly everywhere there is a growing interest in better health and an awareness of the importance of vegetables in the diet.

Unfortunately, there is also concern about soaring food prices. If you share this concern this information is for you. It will help you produce both quality and quantity of fresh vegetables for your table and do so over a longer season. And though it may be hard to believe, only the simplest tools and supplies are needed—no machinery.

Joys of Gardening?

A dictionary definition of a garden suggests a plot of ground devoted to cultivation of useful or ornamental plants. The plots are often fenced . . . , and can be regions of luxuriant vegetation or high cultivation. A gardener is one who lays out, cultivates, or tends gardens. Gardening should be both enjoyable and productive.

But garden soils are generally so low in fertility that crops fail to grow. And even when fortified with animal manures and compost a large percent end in failure. Understandably, many gardeners have second thoughts about gardening when their efforts are disappointing.

A Need and a Solution

Scarcely a day passes in which the news media fail to mention the millions who are underfed and the millions more doomed to die of starvation. There is little doubt that people are hungry and many will indeed die from starvation. The irony is that it need not be! There are garden-size plots of land lying dormant nearly everywhere, but they are not used.

After years of research around the world a simple garden method has been perfected. The method is not limited by poor soils, rocks, hillsides, swamps, city limits, long seasons, short seasons, rain, arid regions, waste land, weeds, lack of powered equipment, or *no* equipment.

The Grow-Bed Garden program outlined in this book will help you to eliminate failures and experience the best in gardening satisfaction and enduring success.

Into Your Grow-Bed Garden Step-by-Step

Choose a sunny location . . .

. . . preferably quite level, and with a southern slope (in the northern hemisphere).

Clear the area of weeds, brush, rocks, etc.

If necessary, develop a satisfactory source of water.

Stake the area for individual Grow-Beds 18″ wide × 30′ long.

allow for 3½′ aisles between the Grow-Beds.

Level each Grow-Bed area by moving soil from the high spots to the low areas; or, take soil from the space between the beds. The 18″ × 30′ strips should be level.

Ridge the sides of the beds. . . .

. . . and maintain a flat area inside the trench 14″ wide.

Flood the trench and let it set overnight before tilling the soil.

Spread 2 pounds "Preplant" fertilizer and 1 pound lime over the trench area. (Refer to the chapter on fertilizer formulas.)

Prepackaged fertilizers are available in some areas.

Spade—or rototill—the trenches to a depth of 8″, mixing soil and fertilizers together thoroughly.

Use a common garden rake to make a good flat seedbed. Ridge the edges again to hold water.

Mark the beds for the space between plants. Plants require living space to develop properly.

Make holes by each mark large enough to hold the roots comfortably without crowding.

Plant each narrow bed with two rows of plants running the length of the beds.

In nearly all cases, only one plant is transplanted into each hole.

After transplanting, give each plant 1 pint (480 grams) of a liquid fertilizer solution. (Refer to the chapter on fertilizer formulas.)

Next, water the new transplants heavily, either by flooding . . .

. . . or by sprinkling. Apply enough water to settle the loose soil in the beds.

Three days later, apply 8 ounces of dry "Weekly Feed" fertilizer in a narrow band between the two rows of plants . . .

. . . and water heavily enough to dissolve the fertilizers. (For the formula refer to the chapter on fertilizer formulas.)

Thereafter, water from time to time just before plants would otherwise wilt, . . .

. . . And feed with the "Weekly Feed" fertilizer every 7 to 10 days.

Apply 8 ounces fertilizer to growing crops at every feeding.

Stop feeding about two weeks before harvesting the crop.

After harvesting the first crop, apply a second application of "Preplant" fertilizer and repeat the steps to prepare for a second crop in the same bed area.

If the weather is mild, planting and harvesting can continue uninterrupted all through the year.

Note: The various steps mentioned above are developed in separate chapters which follow in this book.

Also: The length of the beds can vary in incruments of 5′ to 30′.

Also: The amount of water for a 30′ × 18″ bed surface area is approximately 25 gallons (US) per watering. This will vary with the type of soil and the volume of water when applied.

The Objective

The objective in presenting this book is to outline a simple, inexpensive and easy-to-implement gardening program. As we have all seen, the history of far too many family gardens is filled with shattered hopes, discouragements, and disappointments.

The fact is that the margin between success and failure is really quite narrow, but none need stand in the garden amidst the sad wreck of their hopes.

Trees and shrubs are comparatively easy to grow and maintain. One reason is they are perennials and mature over an extended period of time. Thus they develop a stronger root system. Their requirements for the essential nutrients are not large at any one time and because of the extensive roots they have access to larger areas to search for food.

Vegetable crops, however, are annuals and bi-annuals. They grow fast and mature in a few weeks. Their requirements for the essential nutrients are large and because of a smaller root system and speed of growth, deficiencies show up quickly. If corrective treatment is delayed permanent damage results.

However, this condition need not occur. Vegetable crops respond quickly to treatment and reward the grower with a delicious harvest.

In the past, it may have been possible to plant seed in the ground and with minimal care or concern reap a harvest of some sort. Those days are gone forever. Today nearly all soils have lost the capability to mature crops on their own. The inventory of essential nutrients is too low to satisfy the daily needs of garden plants.

Fortunately, the very rocks and atmosphere are sources of inexhaustable supplies of essential nutrients for growing crops. Those in the atmosphere, carbon, hydrogen, and oxygen, are available to plants automatically. The supply is nearly constant and they seldom, if ever, limit crop growth or yield.

There are at least 13 essential nutrients required by plants. These are found in the rocks and in the air. These man can regulate and the absence or inadequate supply of any one or all of these limits plant response and crop yield.

If all 13 of these are available and in proper balance and supply, plants will do marvelously well on even the most difficult soils—provided, of course, that other factors for normal growth are present.

An experienced grower can recognize by visual symptoms on the plant and/or fruit which chemical or chemicals are lacking or are present in excessive amounts.

It is agreed that the ability of a person to accurately diagnose and treat plant symptoms is the reward for careful attention, practical experience, and continuous observation.

Only a few so-called specialists are privileged to develop his information from actual field experience. Specialists can, however, document their experiences. Such information can substitute to a greater or lesser degree for practical experience by others.

Armed with this information they, too, can experience success once again from the earth.

This plot was deficient in several essential nutrients and the crop failed to develop.

This is another section of the same plot of land which was supplied with the previously lacking essential nutrients.

45

Grow-Bed Gardening in action

Monument Valley, Utah—a Garden Challenge

Monument Valley, Utah, is called by some the eighth wonder of the world.

But few people would disagree with its other reputation for having the poorest of all possible conditions for sustaining plant life.

This community is surrounded with sandstone cliffs, canyons, rock ledges, . . .

. . . and loose red shale.

Desert shrubs barely survive.

The weather is frequently severe.

Dust storms can be violent.

Between our project sponsor's house and rim of the canyon is a narrow strip of shale, red clay, and sandstone rock. The rocks had been removed previously and a rock border built along the edge of the canyon slope to prevent erosion.

Because of the unique setting of the house and unfavorable growing conditions of the area, Dr. Mittleider chose to plant a family garden in the narrow strip between the house and the canyon.

The strip was leveled and 10 Grow-Beds 18″ wide and 10′ to 14′ long were shaped, leveled, and watered.

A variety of common vegetable crops were planted, particularly some that many believed could not be grown in the area.

Drainage was so poor that water stood in the narrow trenches 6 hours after watering before being absorbed.

The pH of the soil was between 7.8 and 8.5, alkaline soil.

Four hours of organized work prepared the beds and planted the garden. Seed germination was good.

Dry granular fertilizer was banded between the two rows of plants.

The even growth of the plants, . . .

. . . and their healthy color, . . .

. . . was due to accuracy in feeding and watering.

The living green color of the crops stood out in bold contrast to the bleak surroundings.

The hot, burning winds and bright, hot sun had no ill effects on any of the crops.

This photo was taken from inside the house through a large window.

Tradition holds that potatoes require a sandy-loam soil, . . .

. . . but here is proof that smooth potatoes will grow in hard, red clay soil.

Sweetcorn was a crop residents of the area had difficulty in growing.

In the Grow-Beds it grew very well without any special attention.

The ears were large and filled with full-size kernels.

The fruit-set on the tomato plants was good even though the weather was very hot.

Bush beans flowered heavily for a number of weeks, . . .

. . . and fresh stringless beans were picked many times.

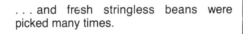

Nearly everyone loves cabbage, . . .

. . . especially when it is picked fresh from the garden.

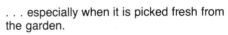

Cantaloupes and crenshaw melons maintained vigorous growth and produced large, sweet fruit.

Several kinds of melons were planted along the ridge of the garden. The vines grew down the canyon slope. Watermelons can be seen hanging on the vines along the slope.

The green garden of healthy crops seen against the crumbling rocks and dry desert surroundings was delightful to behold.

The Monument Valley Grow-Bed garden demonstration puts to rest the tradition . . .

. . . that crops can be grown only on certain soils and weather conditions.

A Primer on Soils and Plant Growth

Most plants were meant to grow in soil and sunshine. Both the type of soil and intensity of the sunshine do affect plant performance, but not to the extent frequently supposed.

Fortunately, vegetable crops will grow in many types of problem soils—even artificial soil media. And they tolerate a reasonable margin in temperature and in intensity of sunshine.

For all practical purposes, plants are dormant (not growing) at 50°F, and some will be killed at 32°F. The ideal growing temperature is between 70° and 90°—an ideal not always realized.

The Ideal Soil

A soil that is easy to till.

A soil that can be worked in early springtime without producing clods or compacting.

A soil that warms up quickly after cold weather and remains cool in hot weather.

A soil that absorbs water quickly and evenly and retains it.

A soil that drains easily—essential to adequate soil oxygen.

A soil that mulches easily and does not crust or crack on the surface.

This ideal soil is seldom realized in actuality but most soils contain portions of the ideal and function surprisingly well in producing crops.

The artificial soils mentioned in other chapters come very near meeting the qualifications of the ideal soil.

The life of plants depends on the soils they grow in!

Soil Testing

Valuable information about soils can be obtained quickly through a soil test. (For detailed information on how to take a soil sample, refer to the book *Food For Everyone,* pages 135 through 141.)

The most valuable figures in a soil test report are salinity and the pH. Salinity deals with the kind and the amount of salt (chemicals) in the soil. The pH determines whether a soil is acid, neutral, or alkaline.

Both of these test readings have a bearing on fertilizing practices.

Soil pH

When plants fail to grow properly one of the first questions asked by a chemist is, "What is the pH of the soil?"

The degree of acidity or alkalinity (pH) may suggest some disorder in the chemical balance of the soil as it relates to plant nutrition.

When a person is not feeling well, the doctor takes his temperature. Measuring the pH of the soil is similar to taking a patient's temperature, in that it may suggest the need for action of some kind.

It may reveal that something is wrong, but it does not tell the nature of the trouble.

The symbol "pH" is just an expression to describe the mineral (chemical) contents of the soil solution.

The "H" has meaning when it is understood that every water solution or mixture of soil and water, is characterized by its content of hydrogen (H) ions and the hydroxyl (OH) group containing hydrogen and oxygen ions.

The pH scale (unit of measure) may be thought of as similar to that on a thermometer. It starts at zero and advances to 14. Seven is the mid-point and neither acid nor alkaline. All figures above seven indicate alkaline reaction. All figures below seven indicate acidity.

The smaller the number below seven the *stronger* the acid solution in the soil. The larger the number above seven the *stronger* the alkalinity of the soil solution.

Every substance dissolved in water, whether in the air or in the soil, is either acid, neutral, or alkaline. And, whether the soil is acid or alkaline has an affect on how plants grow. Good crops can be grown on acid, neutral, and alkaline soils, providing proper fertilization practices are adhered to.

The pH of the soil indicates only the relative strength of the acid or alkaline content of the solution. It does *not* tell the *amount* of acid or alkali in the soil.

For example, apple-cider vinegar has an acid pH content of about 2.0 percent. The percent remains the same whether the volume is one quart or a gallon or 100 gallons. But to neutralize the acid in one gallon of vinegar with lime will require 4 times the amount of lime needed to neutralize that in one quart, and 100 gallons would require 100 times as much.

In a similar way, different soils may have the same pH reading, but differ greatly in the amount of lime required to neutralize them.

For example, a sandy-loam soil containing only 12% clay would require a small application of lime to raise the pH from 5.0 to 6.5, but a clay-loam soil with a clay content of 24% would require about twice as much lime to effect the same change in pH.

Plants perform best when the soil pH is 6.5 to 7.0. If the pH is 6.5 or less, lime should be broadcast on the land to raise the pH to the desired level.

On sandy soils an application of 800 to 1,000 pounds of lime per acre is usually adequate to raise the pH one point, say from 5.5 to 6.5

On clay-soils the application rate is 1200 to 1800 pounds lime per acre to raise the pH one point.

On alkaline soils (pH above 7) sulfur amendments should be used to lower the pH to the desired level. An application of 200 to 300 pounds of sulfur per acre will often lower the pH one point.

Acid soils are formed in areas where the annual rainfall is above 20 inches. Alkaline soils are formed in semi-arid and arid regions where the annual rainfall is less than 18 inches.

The soluble compounds in the soil raise or lower the pH and are called "salt." The sap (plant juice) within plants is a salty solution. If the chemical solutions (salt) in the soil are *stronger* than the solutions within the plant, growth is retarded, stopped—even death can result—depending on the concentration of the solution.

Very briefly, this gives you a little insight into the nature of soils and how they affect plant growth.

Factors Involved in Growing Food

Factors involved in growing vegetable crops are the same all around the world. Wherever vegetation grows there is land, water, sunshine, insects, erosion, wind, rain, cold, etc..

The reason food shortages exist and people are starving is not because there is no land or that crops cannot be grown. There are more serious reasons involving land management.

America and some other countries produce surplus food every year. How? By good soil management practices. Land is one of the most valuable assets of a country or of a family. The prosperity of both depends to a large degree on how the land is managed.

There are six functions which soils are meant to perform for plants:
1. Anchor—hold plant stems upright.
2. Hold moisture.
3. Store essential nutrients for plants.
4. Frequent exchange of oxygen supply.
5. Allow drainage.
6. Buffer the temperature.

As long as all of these are present plant performance is usually good.

A careful study of the list suggests that materials other than soil can be used to substitute for soil. Also, that soils can vary in composition and still support excellent plant growth.

In the book *More Food From Your Garden* is outlined a simple method of gardening using artificial, non-soil materials as a soil medium. It is called the "Grow-Box" method.

The Grow-Box method is unique and the results are well documented. The method has special application to steep hillsides, saline soils, city lots, rocky terrain, and greenhouse production.

The method is highly scientific and accuracy is essential to its high quality and productivity.

After much experience in grow-box production and with a constant search for better and simpler methods for gardens—and a demand for fresh vegetables being especially urgent in many places where land sits idle—the author was compelled to experiment on problem soils by applying the Grow-Box procedures directly to the land. The results were very gratifying and opened the door to a new dimension in food production.

Previous attempts to use many problem soils, commonly available to average gardens, seemed to indicate that the best way to help a lot of people eliminate garden failures was to promote artificial soil mediums and a uniform program of fertilizing and production procedures.

Now with further development, it is clear that when the procedures for growing superior crops in artificial soils are used in Grow-Bed gardening with regular soils the same quality crops can be grown on nearly all natural soils with hardly any exceptions.

The keys to success, in all cases, are healthy plants, balanced nutrients, and some loving care.

The detailed instruction in this book for maximum food production from Grow-Bed gardening will be taken from actual demonstrations conducted in Zimbabwe, Africa, and Halchita, Utah.

The harvests reveal how effective the growing proved to be from the most severe soil conditions that exist anywhere.

Everyone hopes to reap a good harvest with minimum care and expense, so do take courage. *This you can do!*

Seeds and Seedlings

The first step to success is in the seed planted and the quality of the seedlings produced.

Seed can be planted in common garden soil, or in straight sand if necessary. But this is not the best procedure.

Common garden soils are usually poor suppliers of oxygen and are carriers of disease and insects. If regular soil or sand must be used, it should be sterilized.

Here's How To Sterilize Soil or Sand:

1. Spread the soil in an even layer on a flat pan—not more than 1″ deep.
2. Set the oven temperature at 250°F.
3. Place the soil in the oven for 45 minutes.
4. Remove from the oven and stir thoroughly.
5. Put back in the oven another 45 minutes.
6. Remove from the oven and allow to cool.
7. When cold, use at once or store in a clean container for future use.

Simple Greenhouse Tips:

Seedling plants are generally grown in some type of greenhouse. The structure can be small and very simple.

Where the weather is mild it is possible to produce excellent seedlings without a greenhouse.

Usually, a greenhouse, however simple, is a good investment. The objective is to provide protection for germinating seeds and young plants—from extremes in temperature, from wind, pounding rain, insects, and disease.

With the structure you should have tables 30″ high to hold the boxes (flats) of seeds and plants up off the ground.

Level tables with flat tops are essential for growing uniform strong plants.

Plants, like people, require oxygen and light. Therefore, adequate fresh air and light are important to seedlings and daily ventilation in the greenhouse is essential.

If properly constructed, a greenhouse can serve two purposes: a), it can be used to sprout seeds and grow seedlings during cold weather; . . .

and b), later in the season a crop of tomatoes, cucumbers, or melons can be grown.

This type of greenhouse is merely a large "A" frame with an arched roof made of ¾″ plastic pipe.

Clear plastic is pulled over the entire frame. The plastic is held secure with strips of lath nailed securely to the "A" frame.

"A" frames of various sizes can be used effectively to start seeds or plants ahead of the normal growing season.

The plastic frames do not detract from the beauty of a well organized garden.

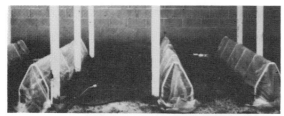

The plastic cover should have a 6″ flap on both sides of the "A" frame at the soil surface. Soil is spread on the flaps to hold the plastic in place over the "A" frames.

As the weather warms in the early spring season the plastic covers can be layed to one side of the frames during sunny days, and can be replaced quickly to protect and cover the plants at night and on cold days.

Very small "A" frames are inexpensive to set up and the same plastic frames can be used for many years. If the plastic covers are folded and stored out of the sun when not in use they too can be used for a number of years.

The low "A" frames protect the young crops from cold wind and increase the soil temperature even during cloudy days. The "A" frames keep the plastic covers off the plants and allow oxygen to move freely within the enclosed area.

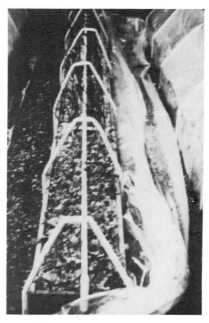

Building an Inexpensive Seedling Greenhouse

Growing plants from seed ahead of the normal planting season has a number of advantages: . . .

. . . the plants are stronger and more vigorous, they mature earlier, produce more uniform and larger yields, cut costs on weed and insect control, etc.

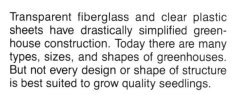

Transparent fiberglass and clear plastic sheets have drastically simplified greenhouse construction. Today there are many types, sizes, and shapes of greenhouses. But not every design or shape of structure is best suited to grow quality seedlings.

This chapter deals with construction of a seedhouse which is simple in design, easy and quick to construct, very inexpensive, and highly functional. This type of construction simplifies growing procedures and produces strong seedlings with minimum effort and reasonable care.

Orientation

Choose a flat, level area, large enough to accomodate the size of structure desired, with additional space to expand if necessary.

Full sunlight is essential. In the northern hemisphere, face the length of the building east and west. This gives the broadside a southern exposure and all the plants get maximum light when the days are short and the sun is farthest south.

Construction

The size can vary to fit the need. Because of the size of our project, this chapter deals with a structure 20' wide × 40' long and 8½' high at the peak. (Yours can be proportionately sized to contain the seedlings you need.) The frame is made of 4 × 4 posts and 4 × 4 stringers. If the posts are pine or fir they should be of treated lumber to resist termites and rotting.

The first step in construction is to clear and level the area. Then set stakes for the 4 × 4 posts. The posts are 10' apart each direction.

The posts for the sides of the building are 8' long and are set in the ground 18" below the level of the floor.

The top of the side posts is 6½′ above the floor level. Stringers 4′ × 4′ × 20′ are nailed on top of the side posts.

For the center row, use 4 × 4 posts that are 10′ long. These too, are set in the soil 18″ below the floor level. The posts are tamped firmly.

NOTE: Before the center posts are set in place, notches 1¼″ × 3¾″ are cut in one side of each post. The notch is down 18″ below the top-end of the posts. When the posts are set in place the notches should face south.

Two rows of 4 × 4 stringers are nailed to the center posts.

One row is nailed on top of the posts.

One row is nailed 18″s below the top.

Before the 2nd row of stringers is nailed to the posts, notch one side of the stringers to match the notches made on the posts. Match the notches to fit into each other and nail securely.

Trays containing seedling plants should *never* be set on the ground. Therefore, tables with flat, level tops, are a vital part of a successful greenhouse operation.

Tables 30″ high × 36″ wide running the full length of the building are made along the side walls. And one table 30″ high × 72″ wide is made down the center. The aisles between the tables are 3½′ wide. (If your seedling greenhouse is smaller, you may skip the center table.)

The tables are built strong and sturdy.

The table legs are 2 × 4 stakes 36″ long, pointed on one end. The table legs are driven into the ground 6″ to 8″.

Each table has two rows of legs (stakes). One row of stakes is 30″ in from the inside edge of the 4 × 4 posts. The other row of legs is in line with the inside edge of the 4 × 4 posts. The space between the legs in the first row is 28″. The space between the legs in the second row is 24″.

The center table is made just like the side tables. There are two rows of legs 30″ away from the center 4 × 4 posts, one row on each side of the posts. A third row of legs is in line with one edge of the 4 × 4 posts. The legs in this row are 24″ apart.

The top-edge of properly placed 2 × 4 table legs is level throughout and in a straight row. The next step is to nail 2 × 4s *on edge* on top of each row of table legs.

To complete the tables, nail 1 × 4 boards 36″ long on top of the 2 × 4s on the side tables, and 1 × 4 boards 72″ long to complete the center table.

Note: Nail the boards across the 2 × 4s. Separate the boards with 1″ space between them.

The table-top boards have a 6″ overhang past the table legs into the aisles.

The roof support of the seedling greenhouse is made of 2×3 wood rafters 10' long. The space between the rafters is 24".

Note: The rafters for the north slope are cut to fit and one end is toe-nailed into the 4×4 stringer at the peak—flush with the top edge. The lower end is nailed on top of the 4×4 stringer—flush with the outside edge.

The studs for the sides of the building are 2×3s 6' long. These are spaced 24" apart to match the roof rafters. The top end of the studs is toe-nailed into the bottom-side of the 4×4 stringers. . . .

…and the bottom-end is nailed to a 1"×8" board which is nailed along the outside edge of the building near the floor level.

Both ends of the 2×4 rafters to make the roof with the south slope are nailed on top of the 4×4 stringers. The ends of the rafters are flush with the sides of the stringers.

The ends of the building are made of 2×3 studs which are cut to fit and nailed in place. The space between the studs is 24", except for the doors.

Doors 30" wide × 6' high are recommended.

Cold winds blow from the northwest or north. Therefore, the door hinges should be installed on the north side of the door frame. When the doors are opened, they will tend to block the wind from blowing on the plants in the greenhouse.

The 18" opening along the length and ridge of the building, just above the south-slope roof is a continuous ventilator. This opening is necessary to control the temperature throughout the greenhouse. This simple ventilator eliminates fans and cooling pads.

Making the Ventilator

Notice the opening at the peak of the greenhouse. The ventilator is open.

To make the ventilator so that it can be opened and closed easily and quickly, start with a piece of clear plastic as long as the building and 24" wide. Using lath or other narrow strips of wood to secure the edge of the plastic strip, nail it securely to the edge of the 4 × 4 top stringer on the *inside* of the greenhouse, just under the peak.

Next, nail the bottom edge of the plastic securely *between* two layers of 2 × 2s (random length), the length of the ventilator. *Do not* nail the 2 × 2 edge to anything—let it hang free.

Next, take a small gauge rope (clothesline). Fasten one end securely to the 2 × 2 edge—in line with the center 4 × 4 posts.

Thread the rope through a metal eye installed in a 2 × 3 rafter overhead on the north-slope roof and about 5' in from one end of the rafter. Allow 4' of slack in the rope and tie a knot on the end.

Next, drive a 4" nail 2" deep into the side of the center 4 × 4 posts. This nail is merely a hook to hold the rope when the ventilator is opened.

Repeat this process at every 4 × 4 center post.

Now, to open the ventilator, just pull on the ropes—one at a time by each post—and hook the ropes on the 4" nails.

(Please notice the open ventilator in the photograph of the plastic-covered greenhouse.)

To close the ventilator just release the ropes from the nails.

Outside tables with flat, level tops 30" high are built in full sun close to the greenhouse. The construction is the same as the tables in the greenhouse. These tables are necessary for "hardening off" the seedlings before they are transplanted into the field or garden.

To strengthen, stabilize, and secure the greenhouse, pieces of lumber such as 1 × 4s 48" to 60" long are used for cross braces. The braces are nailed to the posts, rafters, and stringers.

Paint is optional but highly recommended. It gives a finished appearance, preserves the wood, and increases the light factor in the greenhouse.

Special plastic materials are available to cover greenhouses. The clear plastic is pulled over the top of the building as one sheet. Lath is placed on top of the plastic along the rafters and nailed to the rafters. This secures the plastic.

Plastic-covered greenhouses require some type of shading to lower the temperature and diffuse the bright sunlight during hot weather, or the leaves on young seedlings will scorch from sunburn and the plants will die.

There are several types of synthetic materials available. These can be purchased to fit nearly any size structure, and in various shading percentages. Where temperatures are above 95°F, 62 to 68 percent shade density is recommended.

This type of shading is quick and easy to use. Just pull the shade-cloth over the greenhouse frame—plastic cover and all—in one sheet.

The shade-cloth provides uniform shade throughout the greenhouse and effectively modifies (lowers) the temperature inside the greenhouse.

During hot weather, the temperature in the greenhouse can be stabilized between 80 and 90°F., just by opening the doors and the continuous ventilator and covering the greenhouse with shade-cloth.

During short days and cooler weather plants do best in full light. To accomplish this, just pull off the shade-cloth and store it properly until needed again.

Nearly everyone can build a structure of this design and be proud of their workmanship. The greenhouse is plumb, strong, and solid, with a life expectancy of 20 years continuous use.

What is most important is that the essential factors necessary to grow quality plants with minimum effort . . .

. . . are part of the design and structure.

Media for Starting Plants from Seed

A statement was made earlier that plants are not dependent on regular soil for satisfactory growth and development. There are synthetic and organic materials (frequently going to waste) which can be substituted for soil. In fact, for starting seedlings, are preferred! These may include:

Sawdust—from nearly all kinds of trees. The age of sawdust is not a factor.

Sand—washed concrete sand is quite ideal.

Pine bark, when ground like sawdust, is excellent.

English walnut shells after they are crushed to small size.

Pellet-size styrofoam and coffee hulls.

Perlite (called rock wool), made from granite rock.

Peatmoss (often called sphagnum moss); ground coconut fronds, peanut shells, and others.

In addition to warmth, seeds require oxygen. The materials listed above for use as soil media supply this essential.

The various materials listed work even better if two or more are combined. For example . . .

. . . 40% sawdust, 40% perlite, 20% sand; or . . .

. . . 60% coffee hulls, 40% sand; or . . .

. . . 40% ground pine bark, 30% sand, 30% sawdust; or . . .

. . . 40% peatmoss, 40% sawdust, 20% sand.

Note: When combining the materials, measure the amounts by *volume* not by weight.

Mixing can be done with machinery for large operations, or by hand for family size garden projects.

Also:

The percentages and the materials can be changed.

The availability of the materials and the cost are factors for consideration when selecting products to use.

Some seed such as tomato, cabbage, broccoli, cauliflower, peas, pepper, eggplant, lettuce, etc., can be sprouted in 3 days—or, it may take two to three weeks. Temperature and moisture make the difference. All common garden vegetable crops germinate quickly in soil temperatures between 70 and 80°F..

69

How To Grow Plants from Seed

Fill plastic or wood flats (boxes) with the selected soil medium. Example: 75% sawdust or peatmoss and 25% sand.

The flats can vary in size and shape, but a common size is 18″ × 3″ deep—outside dimensions.

The bottoms and two sides are made of ¼″ thick strips of lumber (called shook). The bottom slats are spaced ¼″ apart. This is to assure drainage and free circulation of air.

Fill a flat, or flats, level-full with the soil medium.

Sprinkle 1½ ounces (45 grams) of the "Preplant" fertilizer over the surface of each flat. (See the chapter on fertilizer formulas.)

Mix the soil and fertilizer together thoroughly.

After mixing, spread the soil evenly over the flat.

Gently and moderately water the soil.

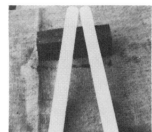

Using a 16″ length of 1″ plastic pipe, or . . .

. . . ¾″ board, make depressions in the flat.

The space between the depressions is about 2″.

Note: Not all seeds are planted the same depth. The size of the seed determines how deep it should be planted.

The rule for depth of seed:

Plant seed 4 times its thickness—not its length. If the seed is very small, double the depth suggested.

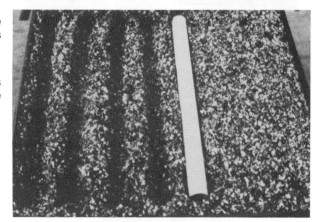

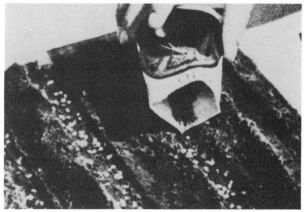

Scatter the seed evenly, in a band, along the bottom of the depressions.
Note: Do not scatter more than 600 to 800 seeds per flat.

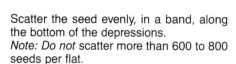

Cover the seed with coarse sand or use some of the soil mixture.

Gently water the flats sufficiently to settle the soil, but do not float the seed to the surface.

Note: Use only water on unsprouted seed. Never water sprouting seeds with any kind of fertilizer solution. All fertilizer solutions are saline (salty). They retard and delay germination and can easily stop the germination.

Cover the planted seedflats with burlap or cheesecloth. Keep the seedflats moist at all times. Whenever the flats need water, water through the burlap covers.

Be vigilant; know when the seeds have sprouted. Remove the covers immediately after the first sprouts appear. This is before the new plants break through the soil surface.

Just before removing the covers, water the flats with a dilute fertilizer solution.

Here's the formula:

Dissolve the "Weekly Feed" fertilizer formula at the rate of 1 ounce per 3 gallons water (US). (Refer to the chapter on fertilizer formulas for the "Weekly Feed" fertilizer formula.) Use a sprinkling can to apply the solution to each sprouted seedflat, . . .

. . . or, make an applicator from a small, empty can.

Here's how!

Cut out the lid on one end of the can. With a hammer and small nail, make at least 120 holes in the other end of the can. Try to make all the holes the same size.

Use the can to dip the contents from a pail of solution and apply it to the seedflats.

Shortly after watering, remove the covers and set the seedflats in full sunlight. This will keep the seedlings from growing leggy (spindly).

New seedlings will be ready to transplant into pots, 7 to 10 days after germination.

All growing plants in the nursery environment should be watered with the fertilizer solution mentioned above every time they are watered, whether they are watered once or twice every day.

Provide sufficient heat when necessary to keep the temperature above 32° minimum and preferably at least 50° during the night hours.

Some crops freeze at 32° and, for all practical purposes, all vegetable crops stop growing at 50°F., or less.

Short, stubby, robust seedlings, require adequate space, light, water, pure air, and essential nutrients.

Problems with Common Soil in Seedflats

Nearly all garden and field soils are depleted of humus. Humus is the fibrous residue that is left from decomposed organic matter. The humus acts like a sponge and a cushion to separate the soil particles. When humus is lacking there is no cushioning affect and the ground sets hard as cement and cracks as it dries out.

In soils like this, water penetration (percolation) is slow and restricted. The oxygen supply in the soil is poor and stale.

Seed that sprout in this type of soil develop roots slowly and growth of the seedlings is retarded. Moreover, root damage occurs when the young plants are taken out of the hard soil during transplanting.

Some Soil Characteristics

Soils vary a lot in their composition and characteristics.

Clay soils, though they may be hard to till, and water penetrates them slowly, do hold water well. Each soil particle is surrounded with a film of moisture. When water is applied the films thicken and the volume of soil expands.

As the clay dries, from evaporation, drainage, or plant use, the films get thinner (shrinks). The soil contracts and cracks. This expansion and contraction of clay soils is injurious to the lengthening roots in the ground. The roots are broken as the soil shrinks.

Clay soils can be improved for seed sprouting by adding 25% to 50% sand (concrete sand) to the soil, mixing it thoroughly. Mixing 25% sawdust, peatmoss, or ground bark with clay soil is equally beneficial.

Mulching the soil surface with straw, lawn clippings, leaves, peanut shells, etc., is another method used to reduce cracking in clay soils and improve drainage. The disadvantages of mulching are primarily esthetic and, more important, it creates potential insect havens. A clean garden is good insurance against insect epidemics.

Sandy soils are good suppliers of soil air, providing drainage is good. Adequate soil air stimulates root growth.

Sandy soils can be improved easily by mixing in 25% to 40% organic or synthetic materials such as peatmoss, sawdust, rice hulls, perlite, coffee hulls, peanut shells, vermiculite, etc.

Mulching and laying sheets of black plastic over the soil surface helps to reduce evaporation losses of soil moisture.

Sandy-loam and clay-loam soils simplify many garden procedures:

a. They are easy to till.
b. They absorb water quite freely and evaporation losses are not excessive.
c. The movement of air in and out of the soil is good.
d. Root growth through the soil is good.
e. Such soils do not crack or set like concrete.
f. Drainage is good unless the water table is too high, in which case the garden beds should be raised at least 8-inches above the surrounding soil level.

These are some of the many types of soil and there are many variations. However, there are very few cases in which the natural ground cannot be used to grow fantastic crops.

The Factors Which Count Most Are:

a. Level of salinity, alkali, sodium, boron, etc.
b. Availability and quality of the water.
c. Drainage—is it adequate for leaching excess salts?
d. Fertility management program.
e. Temperature—either high or low.
f. Production management practices.

Soils never "wear out." The fertility level can rise or fall, depending on soil management practices. Because this is true, high quality and high yield can be achieved in the same soil, repeatedly, for generations.

The Grow-Bed method proves this is true. Because this is so, the major work in developing a garden plot is in the original preparation. Thereafter, the same garden beds are planted and the same results are reaped crop after crop, year after year.

Preplant Fertilizer Formula and Application

Here's The Formula

6 pounds diammonium phosphate (18-46-0) or double or triple superphosphate.

4 pounds potassium—either sulfate or chloride*

4½ pounds ammonium nitrate or 7 pounds ammonium sulfate.

4½ pounds magnesium sulfate (epsom salts).

2 *ounces* boron (as sodium borate), or boric acid.

Spread separately:

11 pounds lime—either agricultural, gypsum, or dolomite.**

This makes a total of 30 pounds of material, enough for 15 18″ × 30′ Grow-Beds (or 2 5′ × 30′ Grow-Boxes).

Fine-tuning the fertilizers

** Where the annual rainfall is *less* than 18″, use gypsum. Where the annual rainfall is *more* than 20″, use agricultural or dolomite lime.

*Where the pH is *above* 7.0, use potassium sulfate, preferably. Where the pH is *below* 7.0, use potassium chloride or potassium nitrate.

... or 2 pounds of the pre-packaged "Preplant" formula.

Preplant Fertilizer Application for Each Grow-Bed

Accurately weigh and spread evenly 1 pound "Preplant" fertilizer, and 1 pound gypsum over each 18″×30′ long Grow-Bed, . . .

Apply the "Preplant" fertilizer before planting each crop, unless the previous crop was not harvested and removed.

Applying the "Preplant" fertilizer is the key to pre-determined plant performance and is a determining factor in whether the crop will be good or poor.

Accuracy in fertilizing produces healthy crops. This is especially true for small plants that are making fast growth.

Special note on gypsum:

Where the "Preplant" fertilizer formula is pre-packaged and sold, leave out the lime wherever the Preplant fertilizer is mentioned in this book since it already contains the necessary lime.

Follow the application rate recommended and omit the lime.

For example: If the application rate is 8 ounces of fertilizer and 12 ounces lime, weigh and apply 1¼ pounds (20 ounces or 600 grams) of the pre-packaged fertilizer, etc..

To be sure the pre-packaged fertilizers are authentic, the bags should carry the name Dr. Mittleider and the trademark. This information on the bags is your guarantee that the formulations are balanced, accurate, and complete.

Transplanting Seedlings

It is recommended that seedlings be transplanted from the sprouting flats into pots. Square plastic pots are preferred to round pots, peat pots, or pots of other materials. Plastic pots can be re-used many times.

Remember, the special seedhouse boxes to contain the pots are called "flats." They vary in size and depth. A convenient size is 18" square × 3" deep. The flats have no lids.

Each flat will hold 72 2" square plastic pots or 81 2" square plastic bands, . . .

. . . or 36 3" square plastic pots, . . .

. . . or, 25 4" square plastic pots.

Transplanting instructions
Before proceeding with transplanting, check the soil in the pots for moisture content.

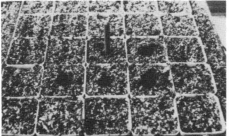

Here's how!
Dibble holes in pots which are watered adequately, will not cave in. The holes are clean.

Dibbles:
To make transplanting easy, take a ½″ dowling rod and cut off pieces 6″ long and point one end.

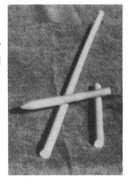

Take the dibble and make a hole in the center of the pot.

The holes should be the full depth of the pot for seedlings with stems, such as tomato, cabbage, broccoli, etc.

Use the dibble to press under the roots and gently loosen the seedlings in the seedflat.

Lift a seedling *by the leaf,* not by the stem, and keep as much soil on the roots as possible.

Select the best shaped and strongest plants for transplanting into pots. Discard the weak plants.

Lower the roots and stem deep in the hole. The hole in the pot should be large enough and deep enough to accommodate the roots and stem of the seedling plant.

Note: Special care should be taken during transplanting to keep the roots from folding upward around the stem like a fish-hook.

Put just one plant in each pot.

Transplant seedlings deep-down to the seedleaves (crown) if possible.

Close the hole around the stem and roots by pushing the dibble on an angle, down beside the plant stem.

Note: Be careful not to injure or bruise the stem of the plant in this process.

Check for soil contact around the plant by gently pulling on the seedleaf. The plant should be tight. Soil contact around the roots is essential for immediate moisture absorption and growth of new roots.

After transplanting, place the flats on a level surface, such as a table. A level surface is important to grow plants that are uniform in size.

Water the pots very soon after transplanting; that is, before they show heavy wilting.

Remember:

The modern concept in watering and feeding seedlings is the "Constant Feed" method. Using this method, plants are *fed* every time they are *watered.*

The "Constant Feed" method is continued throughout the entire time the plants remain in the nursery. (Refer to the chapter on fertilizer formulas for this formula.)

Filling Transplant Pots with Soil

The same special soil materials recommended for planting seed are recommended for filling pots to grow the seedlings.

Note: Filling pots with common garden soil is not recommended.

Here's a fast method to fill the pots with soil:

Fill the flats with square plastic pots placed side by side in the flats.

Put 2 shovelfuls of the special soil over the pots.

Spread the soil over the pots by hand, . . .

. . . and into the corner pots. Do not press(pack) the soil into the pots.

Remove all excess soil by pulling a straight-edge board over the top of the filled pots.

After filling the pots with soil, water the flats gently to settle the loose soil particles.

The soil to fill the pots should be damp. Avoid filling pots with completely dry soil.

The Mittleider Weekly Feeding Formula for "Constant Feed" Plant Nutrition

The "Mittleider Weekly Feeding" formula given below is the fertilizer mixture used in making the "Constant Feed" solution mentioned in the preceeding chapter.

Mittleider "Weekly Feeding" Formula No.1:

9 pounds calcium nitrate
4 pounds ammonium nitrate
1½ pounds diammonium phosphate (18-46-0)
4½ pounds potassium—either sulfate or chloride
6 pounds magnesium sulfate (epsom salts)
8 *ounces* iron sulfate
4 *grams* copper sulfate
8 *grams* zinc sulfate
12 *grams* manganese sulfate
12 *grams* boron (as borax), or 2 grams boric acid.
4 *grams* molybdenum
—as sodium, ammonium, or molybdic acid.

25½ pounds total (strong)

How to make and apply the "Constant Feed" solution

Procure a 25 or 50 gallon drum or similar container that will hold water. Plastic is recommended because it resists corrosion.

For every 25 gallons(US) of solution, accurately weigh 8 to 12 *ounces* . . .
of the "Mittleider Weekly Feeding" formula mentioned above.

Fill the container with water and dissolve the fertilizer.

There are at least two methods which can be used to apply the solution to the plants in the nursery.

One is to apply the solution with a sprinkling can.

Two is to make a simple applicator with an old can. Cut out one end. Use a hammer and small nail to make many small holes (at least 120) in the other end of the can.

Dip the solution from the drum with a pail. Use the can with the holes to apply the contents from the pail to the plants.

Applying the "Constant Feed" solution to seedlings with the perforated can is quick and thorough. A bit of practice may help you to become efficient.

Every time the plants in the nursery are watered the "Constant Feed" solution is used.

Mittleider "Weekly Feeding" Formula No. 2:

5 kgs (11½ pounds) compound 8-14-10
3 kgs (6¾ pounds) ammonium nitrate
1 kg (2¼ pounds) magnesium sulfate
1 kg (2¼ pounds) potassium—either sulfate or chloride
12 grams boron (as sodium borate)

22½ pounds total

Young seedlings will grow very well on Formula No 2. In places where the trace minerals are hard to obtain ingredients for No 2 are usually available. Wherever possible, however, Formula No 1 should be used. This contains all essential nutrients in proper balance and healthy plants will be the result year after year.

When the contents of the drum is down to 2 quarts, empty the drum. Refill the drum with water and add the proper amount of fertilizer.

Note: The "Constant Feed" solution will *not* burn the leaves or injure the most salt sensitive roots or leaves of plants if the fertilizers in the formula have been weighed accurately.

Also, when using this solution it is impossible to over-feed or over-water the plants regardless of the size of the plants.

Why the Mittleider Weekly Feeding Formula Weighs Only Twenty-five and One-half Pounds

Whenever trace minerals (micro-nutrients) are used the amounts required are very small. That's the reason they are called trace minerals. Because of the small amounts (only grams in many cases), weighing and mixing very small batches of fertilizer is neither accurate nor practical, and therefore not recommended.

Caution:

Mixing the separate fertilizer compounds lowers their melting point in many cases. This is because the various compounds are hygroscopic—they readily take up and hold water molecules. Several days after the fertilizers are mixed together they can become damp, even wet, or may set up very hard.

Any such change in the fertilizer mixture does *not* alter or change the potency, but the fertilizer becomes difficult to apply. Although very small batches are not advisable, as mentioned above, they should not be so large they cannot be used up before they become too wet.

Measuring and Mixing Fertilizers

Until the formulas listed here are pre-packaged more extensively and are more readily available through marketing outlets, the various nutrient compounds can be purchased separately and the proper amounts weighed out and mixed together to make the batches suggested.

A small upright (or hanging) scale that has a 25 pound (10 kg) capacity is adequate to weigh the separate compounds—including the lime.

A small 2 ounce (60 grams) capacity postal scale is adequate to weigh the trace (micro-nutrients) minerals—including the boron and molybdenum. Accuracy in weighing and mixing of the compounds is very important.

Note: Store all fertilizer materials in a cool dry place. Avoid storing them in the sun because heat lowers the melting point and the compounds tend to become sticky.

Keep the separate compounds . . .

. . . or, mixed formulas . . .

. . . in closed bags or containers with tight lids. Plastic containers are recommended for storing fertilizer compounds.

Metabolism Mystery:

There is a mystery about the different fertilizers and how they affect plant growth since they are *not* plant foods! Rather, they are raw materials from which plant roots extract essential matter. The particles (granules) which make up the soils function like shelves in grocery markets in which the various *inorganic* fertilizers are stored.

The roots grow into these "shelves" picking up the different dissolved fertilizers which they distribute to all parts of the plant through the plant sap. Inside the plant, these fertilizers are converted into *organic* foods and used for the various functions of the plant.

This is part of the marvelous cycle occuring constantly in nature's laboratory, . . .

. . . and there is a close parallel between the various processes of digestion inside the human body, utilizing the foods we eat, and the action of fertilizers applied to crops.

How To Keep Seedlings Short and Strong

Everyone is anxious to transplant into the garden plants that have many white roots, thick stems, and healthy leaves.

Planting the seed in the nursery can lengthen the growing season by providing plants that are 4 to 8 weeks old by the time the danger of frost is past. Whether or not this is possible depends on the propagating facilities available and whether the seedlings can be grown properly.

Elaborate equipment is not required but the propagating facilities should provide seedlings with adequate light, oxygen, essential nutrients, moisture, and warmth.

To keep plants growing properly, provide enough heat at night to keep the temperature at 50°F. if possible, but at least 32°F. Plant growth is nearly stopped at 50°F.

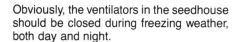

Obviously, the ventilators in the seedhouse should be closed during freezing weather, both day and night.

But during the daytime, when the outside temperature is above 32°F, open the doors and ventilators long enough to allow fresh air to enter the seedhouse and drive out the stale air.

Under normal conditions, seedlings overcome the shock from transplanting into pots in 2 to 3 days and will be growing rapidly 7 to 10 days later.

The usual procedure is to prick out the seedlings from the seedflats and transplant them into 2″ plastic bands or pots. This makes it possible to grow more plants in the limited space in the greenhouse during the cold weather.

The difference between an experienced grower and the beginner is revealed in the quality of the plants he grows. And the type of plants is determined largely by the treatment given the seedlings during the first two or three weeks.

After about 2 or 3 weeks the new leaves begin to touch each other in the small pots.

When this happens, each plant starts vying for light and they begin growing (pulling) towards the light. If this process is allowed to go unchecked the plants will grow weak long stems (called leggy) in just a few days time.

To prevent this from happening, you can move the flats of plants into a colder area and expose them to more fresh air and cooler temperatures, which will slow down plant growth.

Or, you can pinch off the first-set of new (true) leaves.

Pinching off the leaves shocks and stops the plants from growing taller for 7 to 10 days. During this stopped period the stems thicken, which is very desirable.

Or, you can shift (transplant) the plants to larger-size pots thereby giving them more room to grow.

In the first case, plants like cabbage, celery, broccoli, cauliflower, lettuce, red beets, etc., can be moved completely out of the greenhouse after a couple days hardening off in a cool area.

These crops will tolerate light, frosty nights, and the exposure to the crisp, fresh air and cold breeze produces short, heavy, strong, healthy plants.

Such plants can remain in the 2″ pots 2 to 3 weeks longer without injury to the quality of the plants before it becomes necessary to transplant them to the garden beds.

In the second case, the plants should be shifted into larger pots as soon as their leaves begin to touch each other again—about 7 to 10 days after the first pinching.

In the third case, the plants should be shifted from 2″ pots into 3″ or 4″ pots.

In about two weeks, the leaves will again start crowding each other.

After shifting into larger pots the new leaves (2 sets this time) can be pinched off as in the 2nd case.
Note: When pinching off the side leaves do *not* pinch off the growing-tip (called terminal bud). If the terminal bud is pinched off the plant stops growing.

Pinching off the leaves produces thickened stems.

Light is essential to produce strong sturdy growth.

But, once again as the leaves touch each other . . .

. . . the plants should be shifted (transplanted) into larger, 6″ (gallon-size) pots.

Shifting into larger pots should be done gently.

To remove a plant from a pot, place the index and middle finger on each side of the plant stem.

Keep the fingers in place and turn the pot over.

Gently tap the pot against the side of the table or by hand.

If the rootball has the right moisture content it will slip easily from the pot.

Gently turn the rootball over . . .

. . . and lower it into the larger container.

If necessary, put some soil in the pot before lowering the plant in it. The crown of the plant should be flush with the rim of the pot.

Fill the pot with potting soil around the plant and firm it gently with the fingers.

The finished product should look like this.

Thereafter, if the plants are held longer in the greenhouse, the pots (gallons) should be separated (spaced apart) frequently enough to allow plenty of light between the plants as they grow larger.

Adequate light around the plants is essential to keep them short and strong.

Gallon-size potted plants usually require staking and tying to keep them from falling over.

Stakes 30″ long are recommended. Insert the stake into the pot beside the plant stem.

As often as necessary to keep the plant stem growing straight, tie it to the stake. Plastic tape is recommended for this purpose.

Following this procedure, quality, large-size plants can be produced and, in the case of tomatoes, gallon-size plants can lengthen the picking season of vine-ripe fruit by several weeks. In colder areas this makes gardening more fascinating and rewarding.

Basic Rules for Gardening Success

Nearly everyone can experience the thrill of picking fresh, quality vegetables from their gardens which they have helped nature produce.

Like other rewarding and worthwhile pursuits success is certain only when the rules are known and followed. Surprisingly, the basic rules are quite simple but frequently not known or overlooked.

Keep Garden Size Manageable

It can be a commercial project.

It can be a school teaching project.

It can be a community project—working together.

It can be a family garden . . .

. . . or it can be a hobby. The size is optional but consider the following advice.

"Don't bite off more than you can chew" is a basic rule even when growing a garden.

It is better and more rewarding to garden an area that can be managed easily, than to plant a larger area and allow neglect.

High yield and quality from a well-cared-for small area is rewarding. Feeding and watering an over-size area is wearysome and discouraging.

Limit the area to the size which can be cared for comfortably, . . .

. . . within the limits of the time available for a garden.

Eliminate Weeds

Weeds are plants out of place.

They are robbers of essential nutrients and soil moisture.

Weeds are host plants for insects and are carriers of some plant diseases.

Tall weeds crowd and shade low growing vegetables.

One year's weed seed is seven years of weeds.

Destroy all the weeds before planting, including a minimum border area of 5′ around the plot.

Don't give weeds a head start! Prepare the soil as needed—not one or two weeks before planting.

95

Destroy all weeds promptly, that's before they are easy to see.

Keep the aisles weed-free, clean, and dry.

Provide Good Drainage:

Avoid low areas where water collects and stands.

In moderately lower areas, take soil from the aisles to raise the beds before planting.

Make the narrow beds level, even if split-level beds are necessary.

Level the planting area for equalized drainage and for even fertilizing procedures.

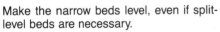

Drain aisles promptly to insure drainage and encourage root growth in the narrow planted area.

Prepare Grow-Beds Carefully

Clear the planting area of everything that will limit or interfere with seedbed preparation.

Clear the aisles (space between the Grow-Beds), make them safe for walking and caring for the crops.

Raise the beds so the planting area is higher than the aisles. This point is especially important on alkaline soils.

Ridge the edges on both sides of the narrow beds and apply excess water to leach out the alkali and excess salinity.

Provide Adequate Light:

Nearly all common vegetable crops require sunlight throughout most of the daytime. Therefore, avoid shade from trees, buildings, rocks, walls, hedges, etc.

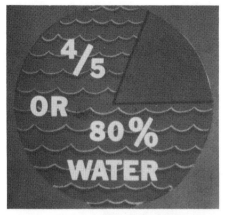

Provide a Good Water Supply

Plants are mostly water—80%.

From the tip of the longest and deepest root in the soil to the tip of the highest leaf, a plant is one continuous water pipe.

    a. Plants require a continuous supply of water.
    b. It is in solution that plants absorb food.
    c. Through transpiration, plants do not overheat in hot weather.
    d. Through evaporation, the leaves liberate oxygen in the presence of sunshine.

A wilting plant has stopped growing and does not grow as long as wilting continues.

    a. Rainwater is the best. Water from wells (boreholes) is generally safe, but not always. Water from dams and rivers is safe for irrigation.
    b. Domestic water is safe to use. The amount of chlorine added to the water does not affect the growth of plants.
    c. Run-off and drainage water should be analyzed to determine whether or not it is safe to use.
    d. Water high in salinity (salt content) should be applied in large enough amounts to push the excess salt content already in the soil below the root area. This practice should be followed with every application of water.

»About Osmosis

The moisture in the ground is saline (salty) in solution.

The sap (juice) in plants is also a saline solution.

Definition of Osmosis

Saline solutions move through a semi-permeable layer (such as the soil or within plants) *from* an area of *lesser* to an area of *greater* (stronger) salt. The chemist calls this process "osmosis."

A careful analysis of this definition gives the key to the way plants absorb moisture through their roots and how to use fertilizers to produce healthy crops.

The definition really says that the plant sap must be stronger in total salt content than the salt content in the soil moisture.

The salt in the soil moisture is the dissolved chemicals and/or the dissolved fertilizers in the soil.

This means that if the salt content of the soil moisture is the same strength as the sap in the plant, the roots cannot absorb the soil moisture and the functions within the plant stop. And, if the salt content in the soil moisture is allowed to increase (get stronger) the sap in the plant will be drawn (pulled) into the soil moisture. When this happens, the plants wilt and if the condition is not corrected death will result.

Osmosis Illustrated

Peel an apple. Remove the core and cut it in 4, or more, pieces. Roll the peeled pieces in sugar (or salt). Place the sugar-coated pieces in a dish. Within 5 minutes there will be sugared apple juice in the bottom of the dish and the pieces will be wet and sticky.

This is what has happened. The juice in the apple pieces is weaker than the sugar the pieces were coated with and the apple juice is moving (being pulled) out of the pieces to the sugar. The sugar will continue pulling the juice until all of it is pulled out of the pieces of apple.

This illustrates osmosis in action. The identical process goes on in the soil.

This also demonstrates clearly how chemicals and any kind of fertilizer (organic or inorganic) can retard and/or kill plants when used in excess. Or how water (called saline) high in alkali, sodium, boron, or other salts, can destroy crops.

It also explains how important adequate, good water and accurate feeding is to the success of any garden undertaking. Further, it is undoubtedly true that good water and proper fertilizing are more important factors than problem soils or temperature changes. «

Use Correct Fertilizers

Granulated dry fertilizer is spread in a band beside the water pipe.

When the water is turned on the fertilizers are dissolved.

Someone has said, "If plants could squeal like hungry pigs, their food needs would be taken care of more accurately." The author believes that many gardeners would feed their crops better if they understood the science of plant nutrition.

Plants can suffer from "hidden-hunger" and from nutrient deficiencies.

"Hidden hunger" is a symptom of problems that retard plant growth but does not produce specific, noticeable symptoms other than reduced growth.

Nutrient deficiencies produce visible symptoms on plant parts and fruit.

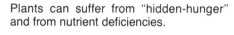

The soil cannot produce beyond its most limiting factor. "Too little or too much" should be avoided. This means that when any specific nutrient is limiting or is in excess, the functions in the plant are adversely affected.

There are 13 essential nutrients which plants require and which man can supply.

Any one of the 13, if not in balance, either lacking or in excess, can result in reduced yield and/or complete crop failure.

Every essential nutrient which plants require and which man can regulate, if deficient, produces predominant symptoms somewhere on the plant. And tell-tale symptoms appear also if there is an excess.

Real gardening satisfaction comes in recognizing these symptoms, diagnosing them accurately, applying corrections and watching the plants respond to the treatment with a living-green color and renewed vigor.

The main purpose in pruning is to increase the light factor in a growing plant, . . .

Make Pruning an Art

Pruning is an art that is learned through observation and practical experience.

. . . to shape it to hold the fruit off the ground, and to increase the plant population in a given area.

For the purpose of this discussion, the instruction on pruning will be limited to taking off the obvious suckers like those growing above—in the apex of each leaf, and all damaged and dead or dying leaves.

Control Insects

A clean garden free from piles of decaying organic matter and weeds is good insurance against insect build-up.

Fast-growing crops suffer less insect damage because of the reduced total number of days from transplanting to harvesting the crop.

Nearly every community has county agricultural agents who are acquainted with the problem insects in their communities. They are eager to assist in control procedures. Call on them.

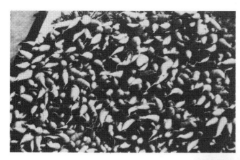

Effective Water Systems

Crisp vegetables cannot be produced without sufficient water. The Grow-Bed method simplifies the chore of watering, reducing it to a matter of minutes.

First, only 25% of the land area is planted. The other 75% is aisle space.

This does not imply that there is a waste of land. On the contrary, the plant roots are growing in a concentrated area where water and balanced fertilizers are adequately supplied.

The above-ground plant parts spread out into the aisles, covering them.

A plant requires living space to produce high yield. Were it not for the wide aisles fewer plants could be grown in the beds without sacrificing both yield and quality.

But the aisles allow the plants to spread out over the ground where light is adequate to make lush growth—so essential for high yield.

Considering the factors which lead to gardening success or failure, the one which influences the results most is watering.

The surest way to avoid the effects of over-watering or under-watering or waste of water is to simplify the procedure.

Here's How!

Convert the garden to Grow-Beds 18″ wide × 30′ long.

Ridging the narrow beds and making them level is all that is really necessary.

But, certainly, wooden frames can be used with equal success.

If used, the frames are filled with a satisfactory soil medium.

Pipe water to each bed.

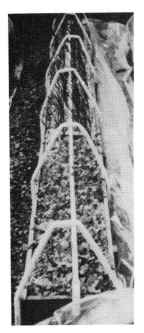

Install a quick shut-off valve at each riser.

Drill three rows of tiny holes (No. 57 steel bit) 4″ apart the length of the ¾″ PVC (200 PSI) pipe.

Before the pipe is drilled it should be spliced to the length of the Grow-Beds.

Thread the pipe into the main pipe (source of water) at each riser.

Lay the pipe down the center of the beds between the plants. The pipe is never removed until the crop is harvested.

Lay the pipe on $2″ \times 8″$ wooden blocks to hold it off the soil.

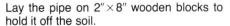

Resting the pipe on the blocks gives better distribution of the water.

Here's How To Drill the Pipe:

Make a jig the length of the pipe (30′). The jig should be straight and level.

Mark the jig every 4″, the full length.

Anchor the pipe in the jig to keep it from moving or turning.

Take a lead pencil and draw a straight line down the center of the pipe to be drilled.

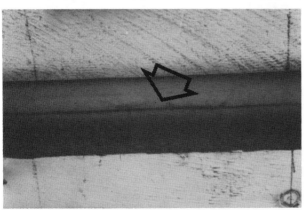

Tighten a No. 57 steel bit (less than 1/16th″) in a small electric drill.

Drill holes along the pencil line in the center of the pipe (every 4″).

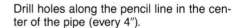

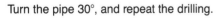

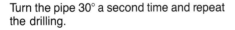

Turn the pipe 30°, and repeat the drilling.

Turn the pipe 30° a second time and repeat the drilling.

Thread the drilled pipe into the water system.

The amount of water delivered through the system is 15 to 25 gallons per minute (depending on the water pressure).

Note: During installation, the holes in the drilled pipes are turned towards the ground. Unnecessary wetting of plant leaves leads to unnecessary fungus troubles.

With this system, a large garden (14 to 20 beds) can be watered in about 20 minutes. It eliminates guessing. No water is wasted in the aisles or elsewhere and all plants are watered evenly—there are no dry spots where plants suffer.

When the quick shut-off valve is turned on the water sprays evenly the full length of the bed.

Installing the system is not complete until trenches are dug, . . .

. . . and the pipes laid in the trenches and covered up.

After the pipes are covered the aisles should be smooth and made safe for traffic.

Once the system is installed, it gives trouble-free service for many years and watering a garden becomes a pleasure. No more hoses to pull or get tangled and injure the plants.

There is another method which is nearly as satisfactory as the drilled pipe system.

Connect a garden hose to a water hydrant. Wrap a rag around the opposite end of the hose. Make several loops and tie the rag securely to the hose. Do not tie the end of the rag, And the rag should extend at least 12″ past the end of the hose.

The rag and the hose can be laid between the plant rows in the beds. The full volume of water can be turned on without erosion problems. The rag breaks the force of the water pressure. The beds are watered quite rapidly.

The hose is moved from one bed to another and as many as 100 30′ Grow-Beds can be watered in 3 hours.

The Grow-Bed method of watering a garden eliminates dry areas completely and keeps the aisles dry.

This reduces the weed problem very substantially. There are less problems with powdery mildew and Botrytus mold—and saves water.

Watering the beds evenly promotes uniform plant growth.

The Solusi Challenge

The soil at Solusi College, Zimbabwe, Africa, was typical in that it was heavily leached and unproductive. Yet, here it was proposed to present the gardening demonstration detailed in the following chapter.

The soil is decomposed sandstone, red and brown in color.

The weather varies from cold to hot to humid and dry. But it seldom gets colder than 32°F. Most of the common vegetable crops can be grown throughout the entire year without frost protection.

For hundreds of years the land supported poor weeds and brush.

Several years previously, approximately 1¼ acres (½ hectar) was planted to sweet potatoes just once, and the crop failed.

The land was labeled "worn-out."

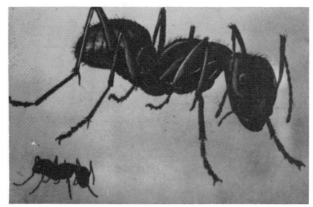

Insects:
There were many insect problems, such as ants, termites, and white grubs.

Nematodes (eel worms) and mole crickets were serious soil pests.

Imported cabbage worms, and fruit flies.

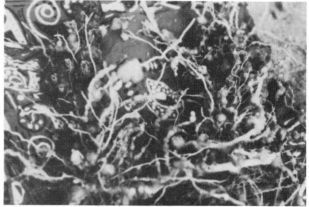

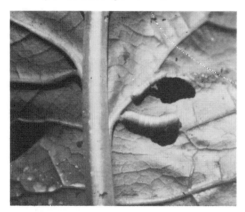

The corn-borer was always active, and aphids.

These were some of the most troublesome insects. They were active throughout the whole year.

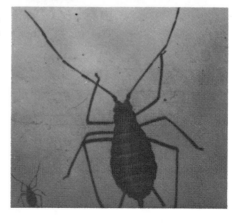

Water was piped and came from a man-made reservoir some 16 miles away.

The purpose in making the demonstration was to supply an answer to three important questions:

Can the average national citizen whose only possessions consist of several oxen and/or goats, with a wife and family, living on some unfertile land, . . .

. . . —if he can speak and read English, can he be trained to grow and harvest healthy, high-yield crops after completing a twelve week training course?

After being trained and he returns to his home, will he use the training to grow his crops, and help others in his area grow better crops?

How long will he use the training and new skills before reverting to traditional methods?

Details of the Solusi Garden Demonstration:

Over a period of 15 months nearly 100 persons, mostly men but also several women, completed the concentrated study and work program at Solusi.

The materials used for the practical portion of the training were mostly of bush origin.

The seeds and fertilizers were available throughout Zimbabwe.

111

The daily training schedule consisted of 2 hours in classroom theory and 5 hours working with the hands on assigned plots growing assorted vegetables from seedlings on through the harvesting. This was the program 5 days per week for 12 consecutive weeks.

Upon the completion of the course, the students sat for a written examination consisting of 250 questions.

The training proved to be very effective, and later, the practical application in their communities was equally effective.

The crops the students produced and their enthusiasm began to disseminate to others far and wide. The following is a typical testimony—

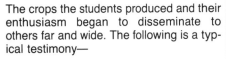

Jerry (one of the trainees) helped a neighbor, who asked him for help to improve his garden.

Later, the wife in thanking Jerry said; "We are going to grow a larger variety and a bigger garden; . . .

" . . . Never, in all my life, have I seen in Africa such healthy crops. . . .

"They taste so good. Thank you for showing us a better way."

And the children said, "We like gardening now!"

The value of the program became clear very soon and a decision was made to put in print the activities of the program as they occured, with the prayer that this generation may yet see *Food for Everyone.*

First Solusi Garden Demonstration

After many years of research and improvement the "Mittleider Training Program" has been shortened from 9 months to 12 weeks.

This report on an actual training program has been prepared to help answer the question, "How does the training program perform when conditions are primitive or less than ideal?

This question is answered in a 12 weeks concentrated course held at Solusi College, Zimbabwe, Africa.

Twenty one men and one woman, some with established families, were selected from several areas in Zimbabwe to take the course. Their formal education was quite meager. But all could read, understand, and speak English.

The land for the practical application of the course was a fenced ½ hectar (about 1 acre).

The acre was flat. The soil sandy, slightly clayey, and red and brown in color.

A crop of annual and perennial weeds, common to the bush, were trying to grow on the land. The soil at Solusi and surrounding areas has a reputation for being leached and too poor for farming operations.

The training schedule consisted of 2 hours classroom theory and 5 hours in the field 5 days per week.

The objectives of the course were to teach improved agricultural methods to village men and women.

Common hand tools consisted of a shovel, fork, rake, dutch hoe, and buckets. Other supplies were string, a scale, some tin cans, small wooden boxes, several hammers, a level, etc.. This constituted the capital investment.

The demonstration in the field began, as all demonstrations do, with irradication of the weeds. No machinery—only hand tools were used to accomplish this.

Zimbabwe weather is generally mild and frequently dry. This made it necessary to pipe water throughout the garden area.

After several days of clearing the land the weeds were removed, water installed, and actual planting procedures began.

Demonstrations are made easy when small plots, called Grow-Beds, are used.

In this demonstration, there were two sizes of beds, 5′ × 30′ beds and 18″ wide × 30′ long beds.

The narrow Grow-Beds were used to grow tomatoes, . . .

. . . cucumbers, . . .

. . . and melons.

All other crops were grown in the wider Grow-Beds.

As fast as time allowed during the clearing of the land of weeds, the 5′ × 30′ soil beds were staked and strings stretched. Strings were used to make the aisles straight.

The training program attaches considerable importance to accuracy and thoroughness. And, because plants will *be* what they are *fed* and the *care* they receive, the amounts of the fertilizers were weighed accurately and applied evenly.

After weighing the preplant fertilizers they were broadcast evenly over the individual plots

The lime was applied first, then the balance of the fertilizers.

Here Is The "Preplant" Fertilizer Formula:

6 kgs	(13 pounds)	dolomite lime
3 kgs	(6½ pounds)	8-14-10
2 kgs	(4½ pounds)	dbl. superphosphate 0-37-0
1 kg	(2¼ pounds)	potassium—either sulfate or chloride
1 kg	(2¼ pounds)	magnesium sulfate
½ kg	(1½ pounds)	ammonium nitrate
2 ounces	(60 grams)	boron—as sodium borate

30 pounds total

Thorough mixing of the fertilizers with the soil is important. Usually one careful blending operation with a shovel or fork, depending on the type of soil, is adequate. The recommended depth is 6″ to 8″.

Note: There is no substitute for a good seedbed! "No amount of scratching after the seed is planted will overcome the ill effects of poor seedbed preparation."

A hand tool called a "rake" is available in most shops and is one of the best tools ever invented for use in preparing a seedbed.

The final mixing and shaping of the beds, prior to planting, . . .

. . . is done with the garden rake. Actual practice in using the rake may be necessary to become skilled with it.

After preparation of the beds was completed they were watered lightly to settle the loose particles of soil. With this accomplished, the plots were ready for seeds or plants.

Actual planting procedures:

Plants, like people, require living space in order to function properly. Through years of experimentation the most ideal spacing between plants has been established for many crops.

Simple, homemade markers were used to give each plant the space needed for best performance. This was accomplished by using two markers with the proper spaced pegs.

Both the length and the width of the beds are marked.

Destructive insects live in many soils and were present at Solusi. These can be destroyed easily at the time of transplanting by making holes for the plants large enough for the roots and stem and applying an insecticidal drench before planting.

This is done by inverting the open end of a small tin can over each mark and pressing it deep into the soil. When the tin is lifted it removes a plug of soil and leaves a hole for the plant.

This operation is followed by pouring a liquid insecticide solution in each hole.

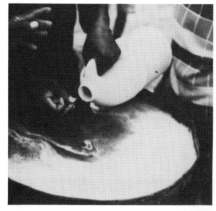

Here is the formula for this solution
Mix together:
240 grams (8 ounces) Diazinon, 30% W.P.
44 gallons (British) water (55 gallons US).
The application rate is one pint (480 grams) of solution per hole.

As soon as the liquid has disappeared from the holes plants can be transplanted into them.

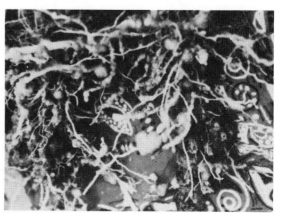

This treatment controls a number of the soil pests but does *not* destroy cutworms or eel-worms, which are commonly called nematodes.

Proper transplanting procedures should take just three motions:

1. Remove the plant from the container.
2. Lower the rootball and stem in the hole.
3. With one motion of the hand fill the hole and firm the soil lightly around the plant.

During, or after planting is completed, each plant is watered with one pint (480 grams) of a fertilizer solution.

Here is the formula for the solution

480 grams (1 pound) compound 8-14-10
240 grams (½ pound) ammonium nitrate
44 gallons water (British), 55 gallons US
Note: In hot weather, newly transplanted plants will wilt for two or three days. This wilting is not injurious, but heavy wilting can result in leaf scorching and should be avoided.

Frequent sprinkling of the leaves of the plants with water during the first two or three days after transplanting minimizes wilting and reduces transplanting shock.

Good drainage is essential for healthy crops and watering every day, if necessary, is recommended unless rains are frequent and adequate.

And to produce fast-growing, crisp, flavor-filled, quality vegetables, they should be fed approximately every 10 days throughout the growing season. The fertilizers used is called the "Weekly Feed" fertilizer mix.

Here is the "Weekly Feed" Formula used at Solusi:

Mix together the following:

5 kgs (11½ apounds) compound 8-14-10
3 kgs (6¾ pounds) ammonium nitrate
1 kg (2¼ pounds) magnesium sulfate
1 kg (2¼ pounds) potassium chloride
12 grams (¼ ounce) boron as sodium borate
4 grams molybdenum as sodium molybdate

22½ pounds total

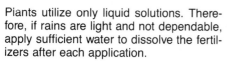

Each time a 5′ × 30′ bed is fertilized, weigh 480 grams (1 pound) of the "Weekly Feed" formula and apply the dry granules over the bed area.

Plants utilize only liquid solutions. Therefore, if rains are light and not dependable, apply sufficient water to dissolve the fertilizers after each application.

Producing Seedling Plants:

The production of healthy vigorous seedling plants is a unique feature of the training program.

The first step in accomplishing this is to select good fresh seed with high viability.

Fresh seed produces fast-growing plants of good quality.

Strong plants are a joy to transplant.

The soil used in sprouting seeds should be clean, free from disease, light in weight, and porous. This allows fast movement of air and good drainage. The materials in which seeds are planted should be very low in fertilizer content.

Here's why! All fertilizers are salt, just as truly as table salt. Even in small concentrations salt delays seed germination.

Planting Seed

The recommended method is to make depressions in the seedflats to the proper depth.

Scatter the seed quite thin in the depressions.

Too many seeds produce weak, leggy seedlings which are hard to transplant and increase transplanting losses.

Cover the seed with clean, medium-coarse sand, or use the regular seedflat soil.

Very small seeds should be barely covered. Medium to large seed should be covered lightly.

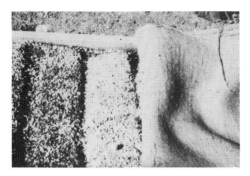

Seeds do *not* require light while germinating. They germinate quickly in temperatures between 70 and 85°F.

While seeds are sprouting they should be kept moist all the time.

Covering seedflats with burlap or cheesecloth is recommended. This reduces moisture loss and increases germination percent.

Some seeds sprout in 24 hours and most of the garden crops sprout in 4 to 8 days.

Newly planted seeds should be inspected carefully every day for new sprouts and should be moved into full light when the first sprouts appear.

And sprouted seeds should be watered promptly with a dilute fertilizer solution.

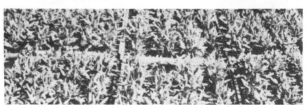

Proper and prompt feeding is essential to produce strong robust seedlings. For the formula of the dilute fertilizer solution refer to the chapter on fertilizer formulas.

Young seedlings are transplanted the first time 5 to 8 days after germinating.

The modern concept, which is fast gaining acceptance, is to transplant seedlings into pots, one plant per pot.

Later, when the plants are transplanted to where they will mature, the rootball is carefully removed from the pot, and if transplanted properly, there is virtually no shock to the plant.

Containers suitable for plants are made of several materials. If made of plastic, the pots are re-usable.

Before transplanting seedlings, gently loosen the soil around the roots in the seedflat, . . .

. . . then lift out the seedlings from the seedflat one at a time.

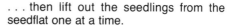

Lift them by the leaf and plant them immediately.

Note: Grasping plants by their stem between the fingers when pricking them from the seedflat is not recommended. The stems are fragile and bruise easily. Bruised stems result in death to the plant.

And, avoid exposing tender roots of the seedlings to wind or bright sun longer than 10 seconds.

Therefore, prick out and transplant one seedling at a time.

And, always plant deep—that's down to the crown of the plant, if possible.

It is a good practice to place the seedflats in full sun two or three days before transplanting. This is to weather-harden the seedlings and reduce shock thus reducing transplanting losses.

Seedhouse: The production of seedlings is quite simple when a regular seedhouse is used. However, where temperatures range between 65 and 85°F., very little special protection is needed.

Tables: Seedling plants at Solusi were grown in full sun without any special equipment, other than tables.

Tables 30" high were used to keep the seedflats off the ground. And tables are essential to produce disease-free plants and also a precaution used to keep plants from being infested with the soil inhabiting eel-worms.

The tables should be level, sturdy, with flat tops. This is to permit even watering and even feeding, which is essential for growing uniform, healthy, strong plants.

If the tables are in full sun, they should be protected from strong winds and frequent wetting of the leaves of fresh transplants with water is necessary for two or three days to keep them from wilting excessively and scorching the leaves.

Earlier, mention was made that newly sprouted seedlings were watered with a dilute fertilizer solution. This same solution is used on all plants in the nursery. The recommended procedure is to water all plants with this solution every time they are watered. This procedure is called the "Constant Feed" method.

Here is the "Constant Feed" Optional Formula

480 grams (1 pound) compound 8-14-10
240 grams (½ pound) ammonium nitrate
44 gallons water (British), or 55 gallons US

Note: The "Weekly Feeding" formula can be substituted in place of this formula. In fact, is recommended.

Rate of application

Dissolve 1½ pounds (720 grams) in 55 US gallons water.

Note: When using the "Constant Feed" method, it is impossible to over-feed or over-water plants in the nursery, regardless of the amount of solution applied during watering, or how often the plants are watered.

Water the plants with the "Constant Feed" solution immediately after transplanting and use enough solution to settle the soil around the roots. This first watering is very important to settle the soil.

127

Soil: The soil used at Solusi for sprouting seeds and for transplanting seedlings in the pots was 60% "copi-soil," 40% sand.

The copi-soil was gathered from between rocks and was approximately 50% leaf-mold and 50% sand.

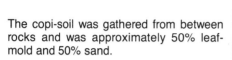

Additional sand was added to the copi-soil. And to each wheelbarrow load of this mixture was added ½ kg (480 grams) lime, and 240 grams (8 ounces) compound 8-14-10. While mixing the soil and fertilizers together, water was added to make a really damp soil.

Transplanted seedlings remained on the tables in the nursery 3 to 5 weeks, depending on the variety and the temperature.

In order to maintain a continuous supply of young plants in the nursery for transplanting to the soil beds after the crops were harvested, seeds were planted every 7 to 10 days.

The nursery phase for producing healthy young plants is vital to the outstanding crops produced in the demonstration.

Visitors and the "Dutch Hoe." Visitors to the garden frequently asked about the weeds. No doubt this was because the demonstrations were conspicuous for being weed-free. Herbicides, which are chemical weed killers, were not used.

Weeds were controlled by hand using a tool called the "dutch hoe." Both the blade and the handle are made of metal.

The blade is sharpened and is pushed so it slides just under the soil surface.

This tool is more effective, and is easier to use than the common hoe.

The "dutch hoe" is *not* used for chopping to cut weeds—it cuts by sliding.

The best time to destroy weeds is when they are tiny. Cut them off as soon as they push through the ground—or even before.

A well-organized garden occupied with healthy vigorous plants and free from weeds gives abundant satisfaction.

129

Practical Field Work:

Daily care of the growing crops at Solusi revolved around the following:

Watering when necessary.

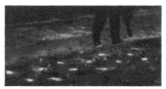

Fertilizing on regular intervals.

Weeding on time.

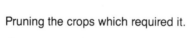

Pruning the crops which required it.

Guiding vining crops to climb strings.

Harvesting on time as the crops matured.

Mixing soil and filling flats or pots.

Growing seedlings from seed.

Preparing soil for seedlings.

Applying a soil drench insecticide to destroy insects.

Protecting some crops from insects and fungus and mildew diseases by spraying with the proper insecticides and fungicides.

Preparing the beds for replanting after crops were harvested.

And replanting the beds as they became available.

The weather at Solusi is favorable for year-round production of most all vegetable crops.

The photos which follow are of the crops at various stages of maturity and also of harvested crops

Large, smooth tubers from healthy vines.

Uniform, heavy crop of bush beans.

Many pickings of tender green beans.

A super crop of pea flowers, . . .

. . . and the tempting flavor of fresh peas.

Uniform crop of nutritous, red beet greens.

Crisp, juicy red beets.

Healthy crop of eggplants.

A large planting of tender green peppers.

Healthy crop of head lettuce.

Crisp and sweet.

Bitterless cauliflower comes from healthy, fast-growing plants.

Adequate fertilizer and water produce uniform plants.

Solid heads of sugar-loaf . . .

. . . and golden acre cabbage.

Large heads of broccoli generally indicate sweet flavor.

Healthy plants produce quality broccoli.

There are many rewards in producing healthy crops and harvesting quality produce.

Healthy vines attract attention of the proud grower.

135

The fruit on healthy vines is large and abundant.

Quality fruit commands the best prices.

When the crop is healthy, harvesting is a pleasure.

Maize (corn) will grow uniform under the right conditions.

Uniform stalks and filled-out ears show proper care and accurate fertilizing.

Dark-green carrot leaves are the results of accurate fertilizing and care.

Long, straight, yellow carrots are crisp and sweet.

Cucumber vines were trained to climb strings to keep the fruit off the ground and to increase the yield.

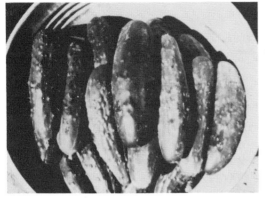

Nearly all vegetable crops can be grown and cared for alike.

A variety of good eating.

The students looked forward with pleasure to harvesting.

You have seen the crops students produced at Solusi during the practical phase of the training program.

You have observed that uniform crops were harvested from land which had a reputation for being "worn-out."

The land at Solusi is typical of the millions of acres that lie dormant around the world, condemned as unfit to produce food to feed the world's hungry millions. And yet, within a period of less than 12 weeks there was a continuous harvest taken from that land.

The student plots produced enough vegetables to feed several hundred students with a surplus to market in the city of Bulawayo.

You know now what made the difference. It was simply supplying the soil with the essential nutrients, water, and some loving care.

137

Comments on the Solusi Success

C. D. Promnitz
Provincial Agricultural Officer,
Matabeleland, South Zimbabwe, Africa
Speaker at the graduation exercises of the class—

. . . When this program was first reported in the press in this country it was headlined as a "miracle" in vegetable growing. I do not believe everything that one reads in the press. I believe that this system is a combination of hard work, common sense, and loving care all put together by one man, Dr. Mittleider.

I was requested to come by my department in order to see what sort of programme was being introduced. I came prepared to be critical as we in this country have been inundated with all sorts of programmes from a variety of organizations and many of these are neither practical nor sound. I left completely converted by the simplicity and soundness of the system, and above all the results.

Dr. Mittleider, no matter how short or how long you stay in this country you have lit a torch which will burn for a long time. . . .

The Chronicle
Bulawayo, Zimbabwe, Africa

Dr. Mittleider is performing what people would have thought to be impossible, developing a vegetable garden on the infertile sandy soil around Solusi College.

(The) "miracle" demonstration plot was . . . to train people from various parts of Zimbabwe to grow their own food without relying on expensive, foreign inputs. . . .

Halchita, Utah, Grow-Bed Demonstration

There are many places where water and soils are much larger problems than at Solusi in Africa, and armed with the successful results of the Solusi demonstrations the author was bold enough to risk his reputation to make a demonstration for the Utah Navajo Development Council (UNDC), at Halchita, in Southern Utah, a place where the problems of growing anything are legion.

The details of the demonstration are recorded here so that all who are willing to put into practice the programs outlined in this book can experience success too, and perhaps even greater than that of the demonstrations. That such may indeed take place is the hope of the author.

Whether people live in sandstone deserts, . . .

. . . monuments of solid sandstone rock, . . .

. . . or barren wastes, they seemingly adapt to their surroundings and live out their normal lives.

Halchita seemed to offer a formidable test of Grow-Bed gardening.

Even after inspecting the land, Dr. Mittleider expressed no doubt that a successful vegetable crop demonstration could be carried out at Halchita.

But a test it was! Several weeks after the demonstration was in progress, even though the crops were doing well, Dr. Mittleider quite freely confessed . . .

. . . that, if he had realized when looking for a demonstration site what the adverse conditions were, he could not have been persuaded to settle for Halchita!

He commented further that in his extensive travels around the world, making crop demonstrations under unusual conditions, Halchita heads the list in having the greatest number of limiting factors affecting plant growth.

This documentation highlights some of the unique problems encountered and will have more significance if it is understood that the demonstration utilized the soil just as it was—no animal manures, no compost, no mulching, and no soil amendments were used, not even sand!

Seedlings for the Project. The seedling plants for the demonstration were grown previously in small plastic pots and were transported by truck to the garden site.

Many goats roamed the area freely. This made it necessary to unload the seedlings in a fenced-in area where water was available.

The potted plants were placed in special wooden flats (boxes) for growing, easy handling, and moving.

And, because the flats were needed to transport the rest of the plants in the demonstration, the pots were removed from the flats and set side by side on the ground.

Young plants require frequent applications of water and fertilizer. The "Weekly Feed" fertilizer was mixed in 55 gallon (US) drums. The solution was used to water and feed the plants.

Much of the land in the Navajo indian reservation is too rocky for crops. The annual rainfall is less than 10 inches.

This rugged area near Mexican Hat, Utah, is called "Navajo Rug" because of the color patterns in the rock formation.

The rock in the distance resembles a Mexican hat and is the symbol that gives the desert village the name "Mexican Hat."

The muddy San Juan River flows through the canyon just outside the Mexican Hat village. The bridge spans the frequently raging San Juan River.

Approximately 1½ miles south of Mexican Hat is the small community called "Halchita."

The land is dry, desert, . . .

. . . with rough, rocky, red clay shale. "Halchita" is the Navajo word for red-rock. There are no shops and no tourist accommodations. The community goes back to the years when uranium processing boomed for a time and then quite abruptly collapsed.

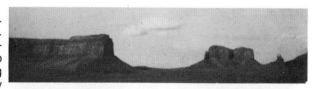

The barren, hard ground was powder dry. The weather was getting hot. An attempt to plow the land failed—but stirred up considerable dust!

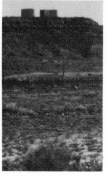

Water for the community is pumped from the San Juan River into storage tanks on the hill.

Two-inch plastic pipe was connected to the water source and used to bring water to the project.

Lateral lines were laid for hose connections at intervals throughout the area.

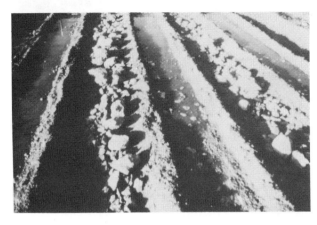

The rugged circumstances at Halchita determined the manner in which the crops would be grown. For example, machinery could not be used because of the hard, dry, rocky, soil.

To conserve precious water, Grow-Beds 18″ wide × 30′ long were made as depressions 5′ apart.

The effort of spading the narrow strips demonstrated just how hard and rocky the land really was!

The Grow-Beds were ridged on both sides and leveled.

The seedlings in the fenced-in area grew surprisingly fast in the warm sunshine. When transplanted in the field they were 5 to 8 weeks old.

Because the seedlings grew so fast, bed preparation in the field was speeded up to accommodate them—before they would grow too large for transplanting.

The beds were marked to give each plant just enough room to grow and mature.

Holes for the plants were made with hand trowels.

During transplanting operations, the plants were gently tapped out of the pots.

The rootball was gently set in the dry hole and soil was pulled against the plant stem. The soil was powder dry.

As fast as the beds were planted, they were watered by flooding to wet the powder-dry soil and keep the plants from wilting.

Over 7,000 assorted vegetable plants were transplanted in the area and less than half of one percent died from transplanting!

The fenced area for the demonstration was nearly one acre (less than ½ hectar).

A garden that has no weeds and has straight aisles and straight rows of plants is inspiring.

Ninety-six Grow-Beds . . .

. . . and 20 standard-size 5′ × 30′ Grow-Boxes (see *More Food from Your Garden*) were planted.

The Grow-Beds were 18″ wide × 30′ long. The aisles between the beds were 3½′ wide for all crops except . . .

. . . squash, cucumbers, and melons. The aisles between the beds for these crops were 8½′ side.

Each Grow-Bed had two rows of plants running the length of the bed.

For crops such as potatoes, corn, and tomatoes, the plants were spaced 8″ apart in the rows.

Lettuce, broccoli, cauliflower, cabbage, and many other crops were planted 14″ apart in the rows.

Vining crops like squash, melons, and cucumbers, were planted 20″ apart in the rows.

An orderly, clean garden demonstration is no accident. The rocks and trash were raked into piles, loaded into a wheelbarrow and dumped outside the fenced area.

Smooth, clean aisles between the beds is good insurance against employee accidents. And a well-kept garden encourages accuracy and efficiency.

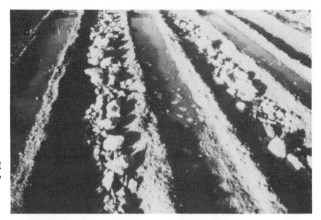

Transplanting into Grow-Beds. The first crops were transplanted in hard, poorly prepared soil.

The drainage of the red, rocky, hard, clay soil, was very, very poor. In fact, so poor, that water remained standing in the beds from 5 to 8 hours after watering.

There were areas in the garden where the soil between the beds was still powder dry even after the beds had been watered heavily for two months.

The first real concern about the outcome of the demonstration was about the poor drainage. It seemed almost certain the young plants would scald from the standing water during the hot sun and high temperatures.

A second concern, associated with the poor drainage, was that the plants would suffocate due to insufficient oxygen to the roots and salinity build-up due to the standing water.

A third concern was about the tomatoes. Generally, the fruit-set on tomatoes is poor when temperatures are above 100°, and from mid-June through August Halchita commonly has temperatures between 104° and 110°F., along with hot, gusty winds. Realizing this would be the case, the plans called for shading the tomato crop to lower the temperature during the hot season. But the frequency of the windy days and strong gusty twisters made open-air shading too difficult to attempt in this demonstration.

The uniform, fast growth and strong healthy plants soon proved these concerns to be invalid.

Because this was a demonstration, quite a large variety of vegetable crops was grown. Their healthy growth offset the many adverse factors in climate, soil, weather, and working conditions.

After one month of growing, all crops stood out in bold contrast to their surroundings.

Here's how the crops looked after four weeks of growing.
Excellent crop of potatoes . . .

. . . and cauliflower plants in hot weather.

Watermelons and cantaloupes grew well.

Broccoli is more heat tolerant than cauliflower.

Notice the uniform growth of the corn and the green color.

Tomato vines . . .

. . . with a fine fruit-set.

Squash and melon vines.

The east end of the area was virtually a pile of rocks, and to show that food could be grown even there, wooden frames called "Grow-Boxes" were constructed there in which to grow crops in artificial soil 8″ deep.

During construction of the Grow-Box frames, picks had to be used to chip away the rocks, to make a level space for the frames.

The wooden frames had to be staked to hold them level and in place. The rocks were so hard they bent the end of the pick.

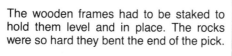

153

Some of the frames were filled with blow-sand and sawdust mixed together.

Later, a number of other frames were filled with coarser sand and sawdust.

Wheelbarrows were used to haul the sawdust to fill the frames.

The growth and performance of the crops in the coarse sand-sawdust mixture was much better than the crops in the sawdust-blowsand combination.

The crops were watered by hand using a "watering wand." The "wand" permits a lot of water to pass through it but cuts the force (volume) to a gentle spray.

The Grow-Box method of gardening emphasizes the fact that excellent gardens can be grown almost anywhere. On almost any kind of adverse conditions.

If properly cared for, the crops are usually very healthy and quality of produce good.

Over-all the crops are uniform in growth. The crops are clean when harvested and yields are high. If deficiencies do occur, they can be corrected easily and quickly.

Grow-Bed Preparation

Soil prepration in the Grow-Beds consisted of spreading an application of a pre-packaged preplant fertilizer mixture.

This was the amount applied to each 18″ × 30′ Grow Bed:
 ¾ kg (1¾ pounds) gypsum
 ½ kg (1¼ pounds) pre-packaged fertilizer
 _____
 3 pounds total

After spreading the fertilizers the beds were spaded and shaped.

During the process of shaping and spading the rocks were removed.

Fertilizing Crops in the Narrow Beds:

The planted beds were fertilized every 7 to 10 days during the growing period.

The fertilizer used was the pre-packaged "Weekly Feed" mixture containing all 13 essential nutrients which plants require and which man can regulate.

Amount of fertilizer applied per feeding. The amount varied between 12 ounces (360 grams) and 1 pound (480 grams), depending on the appearance of the crops.

Fertilizing the plants in the Grow-Beds is made easy, accurate, and fast, by using this simple homemade device. With this instrument the fertilizers are spread evenly in a narrow band between the rows of plants.

Watering the Grow-Beds. Watering is a simple and quick procedure compared with watering the standard 5′ × 30′ wooden frame Grow-Boxes. To utilize the full volume of water and to avoid erosion damage, a rag is wrapped around the water hose several loops and tied securely to the hose. The rag extends at least 12″ past the end of the hose and the end of the rag is *not* tied-it is left open.

The water pushes through the loops of the rag thus breaking the force of the water even when the full volume is turned on.

Watering the beds dissolves the fertilizers, making them available to the plants.

Fertilizers. The mixture of fertilizers used is usually adequate to supply the needs of a growing crop in most soils. But, the Halchita soil required special treatment with several straight fertilizer compounds before healthy, even growth could be maintained.

Deficiency Symptoms

Vegetable crops are quick to indicate by their appearance and shape of the fruit just how they are growing. About 4 weeks after planting in the Grow-Beds, several nutrient deficiencies occurred in rather quick succession.

This is zinc deficiency on beans.

Manganese deficiency on potatoes, . . .

. . . and on zucchini squash.

The peas indicated copper deficiency.

Phosphorus deficiency symptoms appeared on the corn.

Nitrogen deficiency symptoms appeared on the tomatoes.

Corrective Treatment and the Results

The following photos show how the crops with deficiencies, such as this bed of beans, responded to corrective treatment.

Within two weeks after a corrective treatment was given the signs of deficiency were gone.

Later, the crop produced a high yield of fine quality.

Yellow potato leaves are a symptom of manganese deficiency.

After a corrective treatment was applied the yellow leaves turned green and after two weeks all signs of deficiency were gone.

When the crop was harvested the potatoes were weighed.

The yield was 106 pounds from *one* 30 foot row.

The yellow color on the tip-ends of the squash leaves indicated manganese deficiency.

Ten days after corrective treatment with manganese sulfate the leaves turned a healthy green color and all signs of deficiency were gone.

Vegetable crops generally respond quickly to corrective treatment, . . .

. . . provided the deficiencies are recognized early and the corrective treatment applied promptly.

Serious zinc deficiency appeared on the sweet corn.

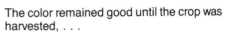

The crop was normal two weeks after corrective treatment.

The color remained good until the crop was harvested, . . .

. . . and the ears were well filled with kernels to the tip-end.

Crops in the Grow-Boxes developed fewer deficiencies than the crops in the hard, rocky soil, and responded faster to corrective treatments. This is a healthy crop of Grow-Box potatoes.

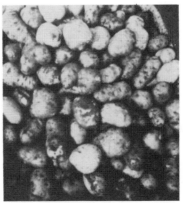

When harvested, the tubers were smooth and uniform in size; clean, and free from knobs.

This crop of Grow-Box beans produced a heavy crop.

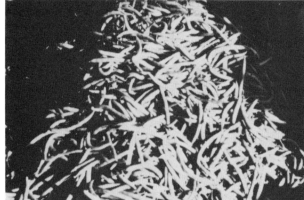

The first picking from one Grow-Box produced this harvest.

A crop of red beets performed well.

This is a sample of the delicious, juicy bulbs harvested.

Young carrots developed both manganese and magnesium deficiencies at a very early age. The proper corrections were made promptly and the crop responded quickly. The leaves took on a deep green color.

When the crop was harvested later, the carrots were straight, the color was a rich orange and the flavor was sweet.

What happens if the treatment is delayed?

This bed of beans had zinc and manganese deficiencies and the corrective treatment was applied too late. The plants are dying and the crop had to be replanted.

Crops After Deficiencies Were Corrected

The yellow patches in the bean crop indicate manganese and zinc deficiencies.

The deficiencies were corrected and this is the crop two weeks after treatment.

The early growth of the potatoes was uniform, and because they were cared for promptly the uniform growth continued throughout the growing period.

Head lettuce in hot July weather.

Leaf lettuce grew surprisingly uniform and fast.

Broccoli plants grew strong and healthy.

Cauliflower too, grew uniformly.

A trial planting of healthy sweetcorn.

Squash and melon vines nearly covered the bare ground between the beds.

Replanting After Harvesting

Within two months after the start of the demonstration some crops were being harvested.

As a crop was harvested, the Grow-Beds were re-fertilized, spaded, and shaped for another crop on the same soil.

This time they were spaded 8″ deep.

Spading deep brought many more rocks to the surface and these were removed.

The beds were properly and carefully prepared.

And, again, the beds were made level and the sides were ridged to hold water evenly.

Halchita had no facilities to grow seedlings from seed, . . .

. . . therefore, seed was planted in the rows. Two rows per bed.

The red clay soil crusted severely, cracked badly, and was not suitable to cover the seed. Because of this, the seed was covered with coarse sand.

The beds were kept moist until the seedlings appeared. Seed germination was good.

New seedlings are like new babies—both need food, promptly.

The regular fertilizing program was started at once.

The second crop in the narrow beds was easier to care for than was the first.

People came to visit the demonstration. Some groups were large. Some groups were small but all were welcome.

Daily care of the crops was enjoyable in anticipation of the harvest. In a short while, harvesting became a regular part of the work program.

Harvest Photos

Head Lettuce.

Leaf lettuce.

Cantaloupes.

Red beets.

New potatoes (from the Grow-Boxes in this picture) were clean when harvested, and very smooth.

Potatoes from the Grow-Bed looked a bit different at first. . . .

. . . When they were dug, the red clay soil had to be scrubbed and washed from every tuber!

The ground was "hard as cement." The beds were never cultivated or re-ridged.

It was a surprise that such a fine crop could develop in such hard soil.

Straight, long, juicy, colorful, sweet carrots.

Healthy bush-bean plants like these . . .

. . . produced abundantly for a number of weeks.

In fact, they produced two separate crops simultaneously.

The heads of Golden Acre cabbage are small but have an excellent flavor.

Nearly everyone enjoys the flavor of vine-ripe tomatoes—picked fresh from the vines.

Considering the hot weather, the fruit-set, size, and shape of the tomatoes was very good.

Fresh vine-ripe tomatoes were picked twice per week.

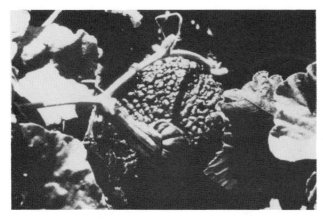

Acorn squash . . .

. . . and banana squash . . .

. . . grew on healthy vines like these.

Watermelons like to grow in hot weather.

They were bright red color inside and the flavor was wonderful.

This crop of sweet corn was buffeted severely many days by gusts of strong, hot winds.

To keep from being blown down the plants grew three sets of adventitious (prop) roots and grew straight and tall in spite of the strong winds.

The ears were well-filled and the flavor was good.

The crops were harvested early in the morning and the produce was sold in the immediate vicinity of Monument Valley, Utah.

Halchita is a rough and rugged area with many adverse growing conditions.

It has many serious factors to limit vegetable production, . . .

. . . but in spite of its nonproductive and barren appearance, and a bad reputation for not growing anything, . . .

. . . there is a spot of green amid the barren surroundings.

Halchita, the most unlikely place in the world to see a garden of vegetables, has experienced a productive and successful garden demonstration!

The rare, but beautiful rainbow in the distance, is a kind of symbol that when properly cared for, even the poorest of soils and harshest environments can be used to provide enough food for mankind to live and to flourish.

What Others Have Said:

Utah Navajo-Baa Hane
"Mr. Stan"

Dr. Mittleider has shown in (the) demonstration garden project at Halchita that it is possible to grow a successful garden despite poor soil conditions. . . .

In four weeks, the barren, rocky plot was transformed into a lush garden that has produced a variety of crops. . . .

Those visiting the project and familiar with the landscape around Halchita stare in disbelief at the seeming oasis that has materialized. . . .

Neat rows of green vegetables are separated by walkways that allow easy access to the plants. . . .

Mittleider used existing soil to prove that even poor soil, strong winds, and high temperatures, are not obstacles to limit production of successful crops if the right techniques are used.

San Juan Record
By Marsha Keele

In the middle of Monument Valley's desert area . . . lush vegetation is flourishing as part of a successful garden demonstration sponsored by the Utah Navajo Development Council (UNDC).

Dr. Mittleider . . . has shown that food can be produced "in the world's worst soil"!

Fertilizer Formulas

Preplant Fertilizer Formula No. 1

 6 pounds, diammonium phosphate 18-46-0; or double or triple superphosphate

 4 pounds, potassium—either sulfate or chloride

 4½ pounds, ammonium nitrate; or 7½ pounds sulfate of ammonium; or 3½ pounds urea

 4½ pounds, magnesium sulfate (epsom salts)

 2 *ounces,* boron—as sodium borate, or 10 grams boric acid

Spread separately:

 11 pounds lime—either dolomite, agricultural lime, or gypsum

 30 pounds total

Note: This size batch is enough fertilizer for 15 18″ × 30′ Grow-Beds or . . .

. . . 2 5′× 30′ Grow-Boxes (see *More Food From Your Garden*), or . . .

. . . 600 lineal feet of row when the fertilizers are spread in the Grow-Beds before tilling.

Also:

 The application rate for each 18″x30′ Grow-Bed is 2 pounds.

About the lime:

 If the rainfall is *less* than 18″ annually, use gypsum.

 If the rainfall is *more* than 20″ annually, use agricultural or dolomite lime.

Preplant Fertilizer Formula No. 2

6 kgs (13 pounds), dolomite lime
3 kgs (6½ pounds), double superphosphate
2 kgs (4½ pounds), potassium—either sulfate or chloride
1 kg (2¼ pounds), magnesium sulfate (epsom salts)
1 kg (2¼ pounds), ammonium nitrate or sulfate
2 ounces (60 grams), boron—as sodium borate

28½ pounds total

Note: Formula No. 1 and Formula No. 2 are both satisfactory. Use them pound for pound.

Mittleider "Weekly Feeding" Formula No. 1

9 pounds, calcium nitrate
4 pounds, ammonium nitrate
1½ pounds, diammonium phosphate 18-46-0
4½ pounds, potassium—either sulfate or chloride
6 pounds, magnesium sulfate (epsom salts)
8 ounces, iron sulfate
4 grams, copper sulfate
8 grams, zinc sulfate
12 grams, manganese sulfate
12 grams, boron as sodium borate or 2 grams boric acid
4 grams, molybdenum

25½ pounds, total batch

Mittleider "Weekly Feeding" Formula No. 2

5 kgs (11½ pounds), compound 8-14-10
3 kgs (6¾ pounds), ammonium nitrate
1 kg (2¼ pounds), magnesium sulfate (epsom salts)
1 kg (2¼ pounds), potassium—either sulfate or chloride
12 grams boron as sodium borate
4 grams molybdenum

22½ pounds total

Note: The demand of the plants for the micro-nutrients (trace minerals) is increasing yearly, but many soils are fortified with sufficient reserves to supply the requirements of many crops for a while.

On new garden plots Formula No. 2 may be satisfactory for several years.

To revive old garden plots Formula No. 1 may be required.

Also:
Use the same application rate pound for pound whether using Formula No. 1 or Formula No. 2.

Application Rate
Use 8 to 10 ounces to feed each 18″ × 30′ Grow-Bed per feeding.
Use 1¼ pounds to feed each 5′ × 30′ Grow-Box area per feeding.

Transplanting Solution

480 grams (1 pound), compound 8-14-10
240 grams (½ pound), ammonium nitrate
55 gallons (US), water (44 gallon British)

Note: For quantities of smaller amounts use 1 *ounce* fertilizer per 3 gallons (US) water. Apply at the same rate as recommended for the drum solution.

Constant Feed Formula

480 grams (1 pound), compound 8-14-10
240 grams (½ pound), ammonium nitrate
55 gallons (US), water (44 gallons British)

*Note:*The Mittleider "Weekly Feed" Formulas No. 1 and No. 2 can be used to substitute for the "Constant Feed" formula.

For smaller quantities of solution, mix the fertilizer at the rate of 1 *ounce* per 3 gallons (US) water—use as recommended.

Diazinon Drench Formula:

Mix Together:

240 grams (8 ounces), Diazinon, 30% W.P.
55 gallons (US), water (44 gallons British)

The application rate is ¾ to 1 pint (480 grams) of solution per plant. This treatment controls a number of the soil pests but does not destroy cutworms or eel-worms—called nematodes.

Deficiency Symptoms for Specific Crops

Nitrogen

Broccoli, cabbage, cauliflower
Young leaves turn pale-green color; older leaves tip-burn and leaves die.

Cucumber
Older leaves and younger leaves have yellowish-green color; stems are slender; fruit light-green to yellow color; gradually pointed at blossom-end.

Lettuce
Leaves are pale-green color; develop brown edge on entire older leaves; "firing" does occur; hearts turn black.

Potato
All leaves are pale-green color; older leaves fade to yellow color, dry and fall off; stems are slender and straight; tubers small and few.

Tomato
General yellowish appearance of leaves; lower leaves turn yellow and dry up; veins of underside on leaves turn purple color; stems are hard and purple; flowers yellow and shed.

Phosphorus

Broccoli, cabbage, cauliflower
Leaves develop dull color; purplish cast underside veins.

Carrots
Leaves have dull-green color with purple cast; petioles are upright; old leaves yellow and die.

Cucumbers

Younger leaves turn dark green; older leaves turn dull green; stems are slender; fruit is dull-green to bronze green color.

Onions

Older leaves wilt, show die-back of leaf tips; green leaves show wilting.

Peas

Few leaves and dull bluish-green color; shoots are few, thin, stunted; pods are ill-shaped and partially filled.

Potato

Leaves roll down, scorch and dry; older leaves fall off; weak growth and spindley; tubers have internal lesions.

Radish

Underside of leaves are reddish-purple color; root development poor; entire plant is stunted.

Tomato

Leaves are green color; underside has purplish color between veins; stems are slender; foliage is thin; growth of plants is poor.

Potassium

Broccoli, cabbage, cauliflower

Recently matured leaves show deep-green color followed by browning of internal areas; browning and scorching ("firing") of leaf edges; heads are puffy and small.

Beans

Leaves show chlorosis with necrotic brown areas at margins and centers of leaves; leaflets cup downward; fruit is imperfect.

Cantaloupe

Recent matured leaves turn light-green color; older leaves develop necrotic and chlorotic spots at margins; stems show longitudinal splitting; fruit splits at flower end.

Carrots

Leaves appear chlorotic; later they brown and dry; growth is poor; roots are spindly and tough.

Corn

Leaves become corrugated; have yellowish-green streaks on older leaves; leaves develop tip and marginal scorch; tip-ends of ears are poorly filled (series of shriveled seeds); plants are weak and may break down (called lodging).

Cucumbers

Half-developed leaves show bluish-green color near veins; older leaf margins show necrosis; medium leaves are crinkled; fruit is constricted at stem-end; growth is poor.

Lettuce

Leaves have dark-green appearance; older leaves show marginal necrosis and interveinal chlorosis.

Peas

Leaves appear dark-green; older and lower leaves show necrosis of margins and between the veins; pods are poorly filled; growth is restricted.

Radish

Leaf margins are pale yellow to brown color; older leaves curl downward; are thick and leathery; stems may show bronze discoloration.

Spinach

Leaves appear chlorotic; margins curl, wither and necrose.

Tomato

Older leaves turn yellow on margins and tips follow with necrosis; dead areas turn brown; stalks are thin; fruit ripens poorly; brown-rot of blossom-end.

Turnips

Leaves appear bluish-green; leaf surface is crinkled and may show chlorosis; older leaves droop and show simultaneous wilt.

Calcium:

Broccoli, cabbage, cauliflower

Leaves roll upward; are ragged and discolored, white in narrow bands; later show necrosis (dead areas) at rims; terminal buds die.

Beans

Death of terminal buds first and, later, death of the plants.

Beets

Leaves are pale-green at margins; curl upward; surface becomes necrotic and ragged; roots are forked and turned.

Cantaloupes

Leaves have light-green blotches; brown specks at margins also in the leaf; plants are stunted; portions of seemingly healthy leaves abruptly collapse, die, and turn brown.

Corn

The tips of the very center of the unfolding leaves gelatinize and when dry, cement together.

Cucumbers

Leaves have yellowish-brown spots; are stiff; margins are light colored; plants are woody and stunted; leaves collapse as in cantloupes.

Radish

Leaves show marginal wilting, necrosis, and rolling up.

Tomato

Terminal growth turns yellow, brown, or purple and necrotic; terminal leaves die; plants lack vigor, are weak and flabby; roots are short, stubby, and brown.

Magnesium:

Broccoli, cabbage, cauliflower
Older leaves show mottling between veins and marbling with tints of orange, red, and purple. The chlorotic spots often drop out; defoliation is premature.

Beets
Older leaves show chlorosis and reddish tints between the veins.

Cantaloupe
Older leaves develop chlorotic and necrotic areas in centers and turn light tan; the spots enlarge and coalesce.

Carrots
Leaves are chlorotic with reddish borders; roots are stunted.

Corn
Older or lower leaves first turn chlorotic at margins and between the veins with a streaked effect followed later with necrosis of the chlorotic areas.

Cucumbers
Older leaves show mottling and chlorosis between veins; veins remain green; leaf edges become brittle and ragged.

Lettuce
Older leaves show mottling and eventually complete yellowing.

Peas
Leaf-tips brown; leaves die.

Peppers
Leaves turn pale green; mottle between the veins; older leaves drop off; plants are small; fruit is scarce.

Radish
Older leaves become chlorotic between the veins.

Tomato

Older leaves show interveinal mottling and chlorosis; petioles become necrotic and etched and tend to hang down the stalk; leaf margins turn up; stalks are slender.

Turnips

Older leaves become chlorotic between veins; sometimes necrosis at margins; reddish tints may appear in advanced stages.

Boron:

Peppers

Leaf veins show scar tissue effect and granulation; older leaves turn yellow at tips; cotyledon leaves are thick, dark green, leathery; terminal buds die and rosette crowns develop.

Radish

Terminal tip dies; leaves are distorted, elongated and discolored; roots show internal darkening; black heart of tubers.

Squash

Stem tips die; young leaves thicken and are contorted; older leaves are dark green and stiff; stems are weak.

Tomato

Terminal shoots curl upward, yellow and die; cotyledons and true leaves of young plants turn purple; vascular tissue appears discolored; because of lateral growth plants look bushy. These finally die back; fruits are frequently covered with darkened or dried areas, especially at blossom-end.

Sulfur

Citrus

New growth bleaches cream-color, then dies.

Manganese

Broccoli, cabbage, cauliflower

Leaves are smaller and yellower than normal; are marked by mottling between veins.

Beans

Young leaves are first to show chlorosis; each leaf showing more; this later turns to necrosis; later the leaves drop and the plant dies.

Beets

Leaves are chlorotic between veins; growth is erect; margins are curled toward upper surfaces.

Cucumbers

Main leaves and younger leaves change from green to yellowish-white between the veins; the region along veins and midrib remain green; blossom buds turn yellow; leaves are small; stems are weak and slender.

Lettuce

Leaves are pale-green; become necrotic; later some definite necrosis develops.

Tomato

Terminal growth can be severely stunted; leaves near shoot growth is stunted, rolled forward and mildly chlorotic; most varieties show small, dark spots along veins, or distributed sporadically on younger leaves.

Molybdenum

Rape, cabbage, broccoli, cauliflower

Leaves develop whiptail appearance; cotyledons often remain green; leaf edges are irregular with portions missing.

Beans

Leaves are pale-green with interveinal mottling; these areas rapidly brown and scorch in the interveinal tissues; green strips remain near midribs and veins after tissue dies.

Cantaloupes

Foliage between veins is pale-green to yellow chlorosis; a narrow, brown scorch appears, followed by severe marginal withering.

Cucumbers

Yellow patches appear on older leaves which become scorched with uprolled margins.

Lettuce

Leaves become pale-green; have marginal cupping and marginal necrosis; under stress, leaves wilt and scorch; plants do not develop marketable hearts.

Radish

Leaves become pale-green; with bright yellow interveinal mottling; cotyledons remain large and green; leaf margins are cupped with marginal necrosis.

Tomato

Leaves become pale, with severe marginal and interveinal mottling; margins turn upward, and leaflets appear rolled; a pale brown scorching begins at the tip of the apical leaflets of the oldest leaf and spreads upward; in bad cases the plant dies; in less severe cases the flowering and fruiting are suppressed in varying degrees.

Copper

Broccoli, cabbage, cauliflower

Leaves become chlorotic; heads fail to form; growth is stunted; entire plant turns cream-color.

Lettuce

Leaves become chlorotic and bleached; bleaching begins at the stem ends and margins; leaves become cupped; heads remain loose; growth is stunted.

Peas

Terminal stem tips become wilted; basal buds remain green with weak lateral growth; flowers abort and no pods form.

Tomato

Very stunted growth of shoots; very, very poor root development; the foliage becomes dark bluish-green in color; leaves curl and flowers fail to form; chlorosis develops; leaves and stems lack firmness.

Zinc

Beans

Leaves and flowers fade in their color and drop off.

Peas

Lower leaves become necrotic at margins and tips; stems are stiff and erect; flowers fail to develop.

Squash

Leaves become mottled with necrotic spots; flowers drop off.

Tomato

Leaves tend to curl downward; become very thick; poor growth.

Corn

Very young leaves develop yellow to orange bands along edges and ribbons of yellow or orange the length of the leaves; yellow bands are visible to the whirl; affected leaves later necrose.

Iron

General description

The leaf veins remain green; the interveinal tissue turns yellow and later necrosis develops.

Chlorine

General description
Unnatural wilting.

Nutrient Deficiencies and Corrections

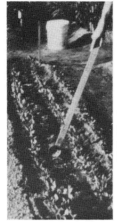

The amount of a fertilizer compound indicated to correct a specific nutrient deficiency is for one 18″ wide x 30′ long Grow-Bed.

The fertilizer compound should be banded evenly between the two rows of plants.

Before the fertilizer is utilized by the plant it must be dissolved. Apply enough water to dissolve the fertilizer promptly after every application.

Nitrogen Deficiency:

Symptoms: general yellowing over entire plant; spindly; stunted growth.

Correction: 8 to 12 ounces ammonium nitrate.

Phosphorus Deficiency:

Symptoms: purplish discoloration of leaves; stunted growth; poor fruit-set; poor quality of fruit.

Correction: 8 to 12 ounces diammonium phosphate (18-46-0)

Potassium & Manganese Deficiency:

Symptoms: "Firing" (death) of edges of older leaves; shriveled seeds in cereal crops; poor quality and flavor of mature crop.

Correction: 8 ounces potassium chloride

Magnesium Deficiency:

Symptoms: Healthy leaves develop light green patches; older leaves have dead areas; older leaves develop bright colors of orange, purple, reds and yellow.

Correction: 1 to 2 pounds magnesium sulfate.

Calcium Deficiency:

Symptoms: Dead terminal buds; poor root growth; death of older leaves; crop failure.

Correction: 1 pound calcium nitrate.

Iron Deficiency:

Symptoms: Yellowing of young leaves including terminal buds; leaf veins remain green.

Correction: 1 pound iron sulfate.

Boron Deficiency:

Symptoms: Death of terminal buds; black heart of tubers; blossom end-rot on tomatoes etc.

Correction: 1 ounce (30 grams) sodium borate.

Zinc Deficiency:

Symptoms: Yellow bands running length of corn leaves; bleached interveinal tissue of leaves; deformed terminal buds.

Correction: 1 pound zinc sulfate.

Manganese Deficiency:

Symptoms: Speckled to full yellow discoloration of young leaves including terminal buds; poor fruit-set and poor quality.
Correction: 1 pound manganese sulfate.

Copper Deficiency:

Symptoms: Bleached leaves between cream color to gray over the entire plant; older leaves die; death of the plant.
Correction: 1 ounce copper sulfate.

Molybdenum Deficiency:

Symptoms: "Whiptail" disease; serrated leaf edges; narrow twisted leaves; missing terminal buds; poor growth; crop failure.

Correction: 4 grams sodium molybdate.

Sulfur Deficiency:

Symptoms: Leaves bleached cream-color to white; older leaves die; stunted growth.

Correction: 4 ounces agricultural sulfur.

Chlorine Deficiency:

Symptoms: Unnatural wilting of plants.
Correction: 8 ounces calcium chloride.

No Deficiencies—*Normal healthy leaves.*

Watch for deficiency symptoms and spot them early. Apply the corrective treatment promptly. For example, the day a deficiency symptom is detected and diagnosed, apply the corrective treatment and water sufficiently to dissolve the fertilizer.

The corrective treatment is in addition to the regular fertilizer and should be applied even though the regular fertilizer has just been applied.

Functions of Plant Food Elements

Nitrogen: Green color; rapid growth; high protein; high yield.

Phosphorus: Early vigor; healthy plants and roots; high quality seed; winter hardiness.

Potassium: Healthy plants; transfer of sugars; production of proteins; high quality of seeds and fruit; increased flavor; winter hardiness.

Calcium: Early root growth, vigor, cell wall formation; seed formation.

Magnesium: Chlorophyll formation; oil and fat formation; carrier of phosphorus into seed; starch translocation.

Sulfur: Root growth; green color; vigor; nodule formation on legumes; seed formation.

Boron: High yield and quality vegetables; root crops; grasses; seed formation.

Copper: Enzyme systems in new tissues.

Zinc: Chlorophyll formation; early growth of annuals.

Manganese: Rapid germination; enzyme systems in seed and new tissues.

Molybdenum: Nitrogen fixation; nitrogen utilization.

Chlorine: Healthy plants; root action in water absorption; turgor.

Iron: Root growth; green color; vigor; enzyme systems in new tissues; high yield; seed formation.

Plant Spacing for Grow-Bed Method

Tractor Row Method Is Usually 18" x 30" Spacing

In the Grow-Bed Method there are usually two rows of plants per bed

Bell pepper, 8"
Red beets, 3"
Peas, 1"
Radishes, 1"
Tomatoes, 8"
Cabbage, 14" to 18"
Lettuce, 14"
Soybeans, 1"
Peanuts, 6"
Potatoes, 8"
Corn, 6 to 8"
Onions, 2 to 3"

Green onions, 1"
Cauliflower, 14 to 18"
Spinach, 8 to 12"
Celery, 12 to 14"
Broccoli, 14 to 18"
Sweet potatoes, 8 to 12"
Carrots, 1"
Squash, 20 to 28"
Bush beans, 1"
Eggplant, 20"
Cucumber, 36" or, if made to climb, 8"
Melons, 20 to 28"

Equivalent Units of Measure

60 drops	=	1 teaspoon
48 teaspoons	=	1 cup
3 teaspoons	=	1 tablespoon
1 tablespoon	=	½ ounce
16 tablespoons	=	1 cup
2 tablespoons	=	1 ounce
1 cup	=	8 ounces
16 fluid ounces	=	2 cups
2 cups	=	1 pint
½ liquid pint	=	1 cup
2 pints	=	1 quart
4 quarts	=	1 gallon
1 pound	=	16 ounces
1 pint	=	1 pound
1 gallon	=	8 pounds
1 mile	=	5,280 ft., or 320 rods
1 acre	=	43,560 sq. ft., or 160 sq. rods.

Fahrenheit and Centigrade

To Change Fahrenheit to Centigrade:
  Subtract 32 degrees and multiply by ⅝.
To Change Centigrade To Fahrenheit:
  Multiply centigrade by ⅘ and add 32 degrees.

Equivalent Rates in Applying Fertilizers:

1 ounce per sq. ft.,	=	2,722.5 pounds per acre.
1 ounce per sq. yard	=	302.5 pounds per acre
1 ounce per 100 sq. ft.,	=	27.2 pounds per acre
1 pound per 1,000 sq. ft.,	=	43.6 pounds per acre
1 pound per acre	=	⅓ ounce per 1,000 sq. ft.,
5 gallons per acre	=	1 pint per 1,000 sq. ft.,
100 gallons per acre	=	2½ gallons per 1,000 sq. ft.,
100 gallons per acre	=	1 quart per 100 sq. ft.,
100 gallons per acre	=	20 pounds per 1,000 sq. ft.,

A Guide to Grow-Bed Topics